CHURCH
AFFAIRS

WATCHMAN NEE

Living Stream Ministry
Anaheim, California • www.lsm.org

First Edition, November 1996.

ISBN 1-57593-804-9

Published by

Living Stream Ministry
2431 W. La Palma Ave., Anaheim, CA 92801 U.S.A.
P. O. Box 2121, Anaheim, CA 92814 U.S.A.

Printed in the United States of America

00 01 02 03 04 05 / 10 9 8 7 6 5 4 3 2

CONTENTS

PREFACE

This book is composed of messages given by Watchman Nee in a training for co-workers and elders at Kuling Mountain in China in 1948. These messages were originally published in Chinese. The English edition is based on the fourth edition of the book which was printed in December 1982 by the Juridical Party of Taiwan Gospel Book Room.

CHAPTER ONE

THE OFFICES IN THE CHURCH

There are only two offices in the church. One is that of a deacon and the other that of an elder or overseer.

DEACONS

In the Bible the work of the deacons is altogether for service; besides service they have no other responsibility. In the church God does not set up the deacons to be the authority. The deacons in the church are altogether for service, for ministering to others. The word *deacon* is the same word in Greek as the word *minister* in the phrase *the minister of the word,* meaning service for taking care of things. Therefore, in English you can call the deacons' responsibility service or ministry.

Please remember that the so-called ministry is service. In Protestant Christianity the Episcopal Church likes to use this English word *ministry;* the Methodist Church likes to use the word *service.* Because the Methodists separated from the Episcopal Church and they feel that the Episcopal Church is too formal, they like to use the less formal word, even though these two are from the same word. All those in the Methodist Church say *service* and only rarely say *ministry.* As the Episcopal Church is a state church and has an official form, it uses *ministry.* In fact, both words refer to service.

Given to Those Who Have
Spiritual Understanding

The office of the deacons in the church is especially for service. Therefore, in the church it is best in the beginning to let all the brothers serve and take care of things. Some brothers, however, are stable, are reliable, and have spiritual weight before the Lord. The church can set these up to be the deacons. All the saints are deacons, but only those who are reliable and who have spiritual weight can be set up as deacons formally. This work is rather ordinary, but this office can be held only by those who are reliable. Only those who are reliable can be called by this name. We do not want the church to change deacons frequently. Therefore, we need to allow only those who are reliable and spiritual and who have spiritual understanding to be deacons.

I hope that when you go to different localities, you will pay attention to this matter. When there are brothers rising up in a locality and you want them to be deacons, do not by any means select those who only know how to do things but lack spiritual understanding. This is the greatest danger and temptation to a worker. Some brothers or sisters are especially gifted in doing things, and you would often like to set them up to be deacons. However, though many people know how to do things, they may want to bring their worldly mentality into the church. Their ability to do things is still in the worldly way. Worldly wisdom and worldly ability are brought into the church by them. Therefore, especially in selecting deacons, do not look only for those who do things diligently, but also for those who have the proper ways to do things.

By all means you should consider whether or not a person indeed has spiritual understanding in the Lord and has value on the spiritual side. Otherwise, worldly means, worldly ways, and worldly skills in doing things will often be brought into the church. Even though things may be handled very smoothly, for the church to be changed into a society by this one will cause a serious problem. Please remember that today we are in the church; therefore, we need to maintain the spiritual standard of the church and cannot lightly allow people to bring worldly skill and worldly wisdom into the church. I hope that the brothers and sisters will not depreciate talent, but neither should they love talent too much. If you are careless, worldly means will be brought into the church, and the future problems will be greater than those that would have occurred if nothing had ever been started. The problems will be so great that it will not be easy to resolve them.

I think the Bible has made the requirements for a deacon quite clear, and there is no need to speak more about the rest of them. I want you to see these two sides. On the one hand, a deacon must be a diligent person who can work with his own hands; on the other hand, he must have spiritual understanding and spiritual feeling. You can let this kind of person be a deacon.

ELDERS

The second office is that of an elder. The office of an elder is also spoken of often in the Bible.

For the Purpose of Taking Care of the Church

The office of the elder is for the purpose of taking care of the church, that is, for administrating the church.

Possibly Being
a Minister of the Word at the Same Time

The elder does not necessarily need to be a gifted person. In other words, he is not necessarily a minister of the word. If he is a minister of the word, he is even more worthy. In the Bible the ministry of the word is one thing, and an office in the church is another thing. The elders belong to the side of the office of the church and are altogether for executing, administrating, and overseeing the whole church. But the eldership is an office. At the same time an elder may or may not be a minister of the word. If he is a minister of the word, he is even more worthy. As Paul says, he is "worthy of double honor" (1 Tim. 5:17). Because he is a minister of the word before God, being apt to teach, and an elder of the church at the same time, he is worthy of double honor.

The Basic Requirement Being Spirituality

The words in the Bible concerning the requirements for an elder are quite clear. There are two things which I wish to point out to the brothers and sisters. The basic requirement of an elder is that he should be one who has understanding in spiritual things. An elder should be a person who has spiritual value, who knows spiritual things, who has spiritual understanding, who knows the way in spiritual things, and whose spiritual course is clear. An elder needs to have considerable experience concerning spiritual things and to know before God what the spiritual condition of other children of God is; then he can take care of the church. On the spiritual side the elders must have this spiritual foundation. In addition, they need God-given abilities and gifts so that they can take care of the affairs of the church and administrate them. Such a person can be an elder of the church before God.

I hope that you will not select an elder for the church who only knows how to handle practical affairs and how to direct things and yet has no spiritual understanding before God. I know that many localities have problems, and the failure is altogether related to selecting those who are famous in the world, who have position, who know how to handle practical affairs, who have ability, and who are experienced in the ways of the world to be elders in the church. Please remember that a person who is capable of handling practical affairs, managing a social organization, and taking care of a family may not necessarily be able to take care of the church. This is because the basic requirement in the church is to be spiritual.

Administrative Experiences Being Useless

There is a brother who has twenty years of administrative experience. Many brothers have come and asked me, "Why not ask that brother to be an elder?" I said, "His twenty years of administrative experience do not count as even one year in the church. They are useless. Even though he is a good Christian, he does not have enough understanding concerning spiritual things." The church is spiritual, and a person must have spiritual weight before God. He must have spiritual ways and a condition of being spiritual in order to be an elder; otherwise, if this brother were to come in, he would produce problems immediately.

We would rather select one who has spiritual weight, even if he has no ability in handling practical affairs. Of course, it is best for him to have both aspects: to know the spiritual things and also to be able to handle practical affairs. If a person does not know how to manage his own household, how can he take care of the church of God? But this is only half of the matter. Does this mean that a person who can manage his own household can take care of the house of God? No, it does not! Being spiritual is the foundation. Not everyone who can manage his own household can take care of the church of God. Many people can manage their household well, but they are not even saved. Can we then invite them to take care of the church? Only one who has a way in spiritual things and who can also manage his household can be an elder and administrate the church of God.

Therefore, when you select a responsible brother, always select one who has spiritual weight, who has spiritual ways, and who does not easily become proud, overly excited, or puffed up. The life of this person before God needs to be reliable. Select one whose life is reliable, but do not select anyone who is proud. Select one who is stable, but not the so-called genius. On the spiritual side this person should be stable and firm, having spiritual insight, spiritual knowledge, and spiritual understanding before God. Only such a person can be selected.

Able to Manage His Own Household

After you have three, five, seven, or eight such people, you still have to examine them in the aspect of managing practical affairs. The one who can manage and administrate can be an overseer. If a person cannot manage his own household, he cannot take care of the church.

If the church were like a worldly organization, we would need to select only those who have ability. But the church is a spiritual organization; therefore, you must first take care of the question of spirituality and then look at the ability, at whether or not a particular one can take care of practical affairs. If he cannot manage practical affairs, neither can he be an elder. Only one who has knowledge in spiritual things and possesses ability in handling practical affairs will have very little problem in the church, and his condition will be quite reliable. Otherwise, he will be able to handle practical affairs, but he will cause damage on the spiritual side. That would not be right.

An Example

A brother, who has passed away, was an elder of a Christian group. During our early days in Shanghai, he often came to my place to talk. He was a good brother and really capable in handling practical affairs, and he was also zealous. But he had very little understanding in spiritual things, if any, and he was even more lacking in spiritual experience. One day he came to talk with me and said, "A sister among us sinned and cried loudly in the meeting. Mr. Nee, don't you think that is funny?" After he finished speaking, he sat there and began to laugh loudly. An elder in a church considered it a laughable matter to see a sister confess her sins and cry. You can realize then his spiritual condition. Of course, he was the best in his group, but he could not bear responsibility in the church. He himself had never confessed his sins or wept to such an extent, so naturally he considered it funny when he saw someone weeping one day.

I am only citing an example. There may be several hundred cases like this in the church. To weep for your sins is an elementary matter in spiritual life, but this brother did not understand this at all. What shall we do if he also laughs at many other spiritual actions related to us? Such a one feels that all the spiritual things are strange and laughable and cannot comprehend one spiritual thing at all. If he becomes an elder, the church is finished with regard to its spiritual path.

Therefore, as to the requirements for an elder, the first relates to spiritual things, to spiritual understanding, and to spiritual experience.

To be an elder, a person also needs to be reliable. Do not consider someone who behaves like a drunkard, wandering around doing nothing. Sometimes his condition is good and at other times it is bad. Such a person cannot manage the church. The one who manages the church must be quite stable and quite reliable. At the same time, he should also be able to manage his own household. Without this, he is not qualified.

Therefore, do not reverse the foundation and the building.

Do not select a person who can handle only practical affairs well. Such a person can be a deacon at the most, but never an elder. At the most he can be one who only receives instructions in the church; he cannot give instructions.

The Exclusive Responsibility of the Church Being the Care of Spiritual Matters

Perhaps I can give another illustration. Suppose that today you meet a very intelligent and capable person. If he goes to work in a hospital, at the most you can ask him to handle practical affairs, but you cannot ask him to be the chief physician. At the most you can ask him to manage business affairs, but not to diagnose diseases. A hospital is a professional organization, not a business organization. There may be a person in a business school who is very intelligent and very capable of handling things, but you cannot ask him to be a dean, a principal, or a department chairman immediately. At the most you can invite him to take care of only general affairs, because the other positions are specialized and can be held only by those who have special knowledge.

There may be a very bright person in a business corporation, but you cannot ask him to be the manager of business operations immediately, because business operations are specialized. Similarly, the church is an organization that specializes in spiritual things. Therefore, you may ask only those who know the trade to do the job.

You need to know that the church is spiritual and that practical affairs are only secondary. Therefore, when you select an elder in a certain locality, you should first consider him from the spiritual viewpoint. Afterward, you have to see whether or not he knows how to direct, oversee, and lead. This brother must be one who has insight and knowledge in spiritual things, who has been built up in them, and who also has the capability in practical affairs. Then, when there are spiritual matters, he will not cause problems. Therefore, I hope the brothers will pay special attention to these things. Do not lightly select a person to be an elder. When you make a selection, pay attention to the spiritual aspect first, and then pay attention to the practical aspect.

Giving Help to the Elders

When you go out, your responsibility is great. For what reason? You will remember that Paul lived in Ephesus for a period of time and that there were elders there (Acts 20). However, while Paul was living in Ephesus, he granted the elders much help. Therefore, when he left, he could say these words to the elders: "Take heed...among whom the Holy Spirit has placed you as overseers" (v. 28). Paul personally imparted spiritual help to the elders. He did not merely appoint them and hand things over to them and then stop there. Paul continued to help them and to teach them how to be elders.

Later, Paul left Timothy in Ephesus and Titus in Crete and charged them to appoint elders. If you read the first Epistle to Timothy and the Epistle to Titus, you will see that it was not merely a matter of appointing elders and then stopping there, but also of helping the elders to serve together along with them. Paul charged these two young apostles, Timothy and Titus, to appoint elders in the churches and to guide them in their serving. In the first Epistle to Timothy and the Epistle to Titus, there are several charges like this. If you have time to read these Epistles, you will see that Paul charged Timothy and Titus to work together with the elders in the church. "These things I write to you....But if I delay, I write that you may know how one ought to conduct himself in the house of God" (1 Tim. 3:14-15).

What is the significance here? If you appoint elders in a locality, you cannot assume that once you have appointed them your job is done. You also cannot assume that you can let them go on by themselves since all of the responsibilities are in their hands, that is, let them make mistakes by themselves. Rather, after you have appointed elders in a locality, you need to observe how they go on, and you need to help them. In many things you need to teach them and watch them. Only then can you again appoint, arrange, and teach elders in another place. Otherwise, a local church is at a standstill once it is set up. Here is a group of people who have never taken care of the affairs of the church. Although they have some spiritual experience, they do not know how to handle the affairs of the church. It would be strange to expect such inexperienced ones not to make mistakes.

Therefore, today your responsibility is great. At every opportunity you need to help the elders learn to be proper elders. Many people in their daily life speak lightly and make jokes. When they come to the church and serve, they also speak lightly and make jokes. So you need to help them. Every time their attitude becomes loose or light, you need to say, "Brothers, this is a spiritual matter, and this is something before God. You should not speak in a loose way and laugh like this." Thus, you stop this. When some people do their job in the world, they speak lightly and criticize loosely. Then they bring this habit into the church. Whenever you hear criticism or loose talk, you should say, "Here you need to obey and not give your opinions. We do not need to give opinions, but we need to learn to obey." Thus, you stop this.

In their spiritual service some may resort to manipulation or maneuvering. In such a case, you should tell them, "Brothers, among God's children we do not manipulate, nor do we maneuver. We deal with situations; we do not avoid them." Those who are able to deal with issues before God can be elders, not those who are able to avoid issues.

Some people may have long been in a position of being the head of a household or a master; therefore, their attitude is quite hard, their words impolite, and their spirits not tender. You need to help them see that their words should be strong and firm but that their spirit should be tender. They need both in order to take care of church affairs.

These are all details, but they are basic. It would be too poor if the elders in the church were afraid of problems and tried to avoid them. It would also be poor if the elders always manipulated things in the church, holding back what needed to be spoken and failing to rebuke when it was needed. People like this cannot be elders. This does not mean that an elder in the church should always look for causes to be angry or for things to rebuke or that he should handle church affairs with harshness. The church needs a person whose spirit is broken before God, who has been smitten by God, who has no personal feeling, and who is soft before God yet firm in handling things.

You need to frequently help the brothers in this way. Then spontaneously when they come to the church, they will not be careless. Their harshness will not be brought into the church. They need to know that they are in the church and not in their home or in an office. We need to use spiritual words to guide them step by step. After a period of time they will be able to take care of the church properly.

THE MEETING OF THE OVERSEERS

In every locality all the responsible brothers (those who are elders and overseers) should have an overseers' meeting every week. You can give this meeting any name. You may call it the overseers' meeting or a shepherding meeting. This is the time for the responsible brothers to pray together and to receive the brothers and sisters. This is something they must do.

I know of a certain church (not in China) where the responsible brothers decided to meet for a whole day once a week. Starting in the morning, everyone brought his food and labored together to pray and consider every item of the things in the church.

Perhaps we may not have that much time; then at least once a week the leading brothers should meet together for half a day or a few hours.

Considering Things before God
during the First Half of the Meeting

During the first half of the meeting (perhaps after lunch from 1:00 p.m. to 2:00, 3:00, or 4:00 p.m.), the elders should close their doors and not care for anything else but the affairs of the church. Seriously consider and arrange things before God and discuss them item by item. Sometimes you can also have discussions like those in 1 Corinthians 14 to fellowship the light that you have received. However, do not make decisions based upon your discussions. In the Bible there are discussions in order to deal with things, but discussion is for seeking light and not for making decisions. Discussion is to discover facts and lay them out but not for making decisions. During that time the brothers should discuss, consider, and pray over all the things item by item.

Receiving Brothers
during the Second Half of the Meeting

During the second half of the meeting, set aside a time to receive brothers. You should wait there whether or not brothers come to see you. We must by all means set aside time to receive the brothers and sisters. This will be helpful to the work and to the church.

The Workers Meeting Together with the Overseers

At the same time you workers should stand beside the elders and be with them. In that day or half day, you should be with them and watch them. There are things you need to tell them. Their light attitude should be corrected. Their attitude should be proper. Remind them that they are dealing with spiritual matters. When people come to ask questions, teach the elders how to answer and how to explain. In the beginning you may answer when some brothers come to ask questions. After those brothers leave, tell the elders why you answered in that way, why you said it in those words, what scriptural basis you have, and what feeling you have. In some cases you may need to rebuke a brother who comes. When that brother leaves, you need to tell them why you rebuked him. After a period of time, let them handle it and sit back and watch.

Producing a Few Reliable, Responsible Brothers

We believe that when everyone serves, this is the church. The church service is the service of the Body. It is not a matter of two or three persons serving, but the whole church serving. Therefore, when you go out to work, it would be a big mistake if you could not cause all the brothers to come forth to serve. When you go out, you may lead many to be saved and bring them into service, yet if you cannot produce a few reliable brothers to bear the responsibility of the church, your going out will be a total failure. I hope that when you go out this time, you will be very busy. But do not be busy in an ordinary way, because there is much work you have to initiate. There is a great amount of work for you to do. It is all before you. One item of this work is to produce a few responsible brothers in each locality. By no means should you work in a way that only you yourself know how to bear responsibility, yet you are not able to help others do so.

The principle of the church is that the Lord Jesus put Himself in the twelve, the twelve in the three thousand, and the three thousand in tens of thousands. You put yourself in many responsible brothers, the responsible brothers in many brothers and sisters, and many brothers and sisters in many sinners. You should continue to spread in such a way. Perhaps when you come back to Kuling after many years, you will have grown spiritually. But if you cannot reproduce your growth in three, five, eight, or ten brothers, I will recognize this as a grave failure in your service.

Therefore, you should cause the elders of the local churches to be capable of bearing responsibility. Paul did not leave Titus in Crete and Timothy in Ephesus and tell them to return after they established elders. Rather, he told them to set up elders and to teach and train the elders how to be proper elders, helping them to an extent that they could bear responsibility before God. Then the way was opened.

Therefore, I hope that from now on you will be very busy. I hope that no one will be lazy. A lazy person is useless. Always put yourself in the midst of the responsible brothers and help them to the extent that they can bear responsibility. However, your own spiritual condition must be more advanced than theirs. Otherwise, you will not be able to meet the need.

I hope that you brothers can properly deal with this matter of the responsible brothers and train them properly. Pay attention to the aspect of responsibility and oversight step by step.

Showing Them How to Do the Work

The regular meeting of the responsible brothers is a very important item of their training. In this meeting show them how to do the work. If you go to a place and live for three months (those who travel often for the work need to pay special attention to this), you need to arrange a time to gather all the responsible brothers together, perhaps on Friday or Saturday for an entire day or half a day, to help them take care of the affairs of the church. You should put all the weekly affairs of the church together for fellowship and prayer. During that time you should not receive people. The first half of that time is the time for you to take care of affairs before God. Lock yourselves inside the room as those who have run into a cave and shut themselves up. During the first half, no one should be allowed to come in. No one should even be allowed to come in to report things to you. Let the brothers and sisters know that this is the time the responsible brothers are dealing with things before God, and no one should come in. They can knock on the door only if the house is on fire and only when the fire has burned to the floor; even then they still should not come too early. This is the time the responsible brothers are dealing with matters before God, just as Moses and Joshua were doing on the mountain. You need to take proper care of the affairs there.

After the affairs are taken care of, go and inform the deacons that certain matters need to be taken care of this week. You need to go personally and assign the things. Certain matters are to be announced to the saints, and certain matters should be assigned to the brothers for them to carry out.

In handling the affairs of the church, you must be able to manage first and know how to watch and oversee second. Do not be passive. At least in the early phase be active; oversee and manage. When the brothers and sisters become strong, you can ask them to take care of the affairs of the church. This is how the church should be. In the first phase do not put things in their hands right away. When you go out, always give yourself to the responsible brothers in each locality, and they should in turn give themselves to the local brothers.

Always make the meeting of the overseers very solemn. Charge them to shut themselves inside during this period for two or three hours before God and not receive any brother nor talk about anyone. Bring the things of this week before God item by item to see how they should be done. After these things are taken care of, certain matters have to be made known to the brothers, and certain matters have to be made known to the deacons. Afterwards, set aside two or three hours for receiving the local brothers. If there are more people, set aside more time; if there are fewer people, less time. During this time, if the brothers and sisters want to look for the elders of the church, they will be able to find them. Not only would one elder be there, but all the elders would be there.

In the early phase, you should take care of this meeting of the overseers in an active way. In the later phase, you should cause the brothers to become active, and they should go forward. In that meeting you should show the responsible brothers how to deal with affairs and what scriptural basis you have to deal in such a way. Encourage them and also restrict them. You should be observant. Whenever you see that something is wrong, you need to say, "Brother, this is not allowed!" When you see that something is right, you should say, "Brother, this is right!"

All the Brothers and Sisters Serving
Being the Church

Therefore, when you go out this time, you should be very busy. Put yourself into the work and also encourage others to participate. You need to labor until the day comes when all the brothers and sisters come forth to serve, all the saints participate, everyone serves God, and everyone is a priest. Then you will truly see what the church is.

I do not know whether or not you have seen this way. You have to understand this way. The way depends on you. You should give yourself to a number of people, and they in turn should give themselves to all the brothers and sisters. All the brothers and sisters then go out. To practice this is the way of the church. If there is the office of eldership in the church but the brothers and sisters are passive, then please remember that at this time it is no longer a church but a denomination. Therefore, brothers, when you go out to work, if you cannot reach the last step, the final step of causing all the brothers and sisters to rise up to serve God and bear responsibility in church affairs, you have totally failed, because that is not the church. Please remember the way you should take: you should give yourself to the elders. Then you need to show the elders that no matter how hard they try, they are too few to be able to handle the affairs of the church properly. They are only overseers and should not try to do everything themselves. They should not replace the church to do everything; rather, they should oversee the church to do everything. It is not a matter of doing it by themselves, but a matter of overseeing, watching, encouraging, and teaching them to do it, and causing everyone in the church to participate. At such a time you have the reality of the church.

The Meeting of the Overseers Being the Source of Things

When the responsible brothers in each locality are gradually manifested, or when any locality already has responsible brothers, they should meet together. Every week the responsible brothers in a locality should meet. When that meeting is strong, they will be able to lead the brothers. This is a very important matter. The meeting of the responsible brothers is the source of many things. Many things can be initiated from that meeting. When people come to that meeting, many problems will be solved. After the brothers have taken care of many situations before God, the second half of the meeting is the time to receive the saints. Then the saints will realize that these overseers' meetings are not light or unimportant. Therefore, we need to walk the way ahead of us properly before God. We need to maintain this meeting of the overseers before God. Take care of this meeting properly so that everyone can receive help one by one.

The Epistles to Timothy and Titus

Read 1 and 2 Timothy and the Epistle to Titus again. See how God charged them to lead. You should learn from these Epistles how to help the elders and cause them to realize that they should not replace the whole Body, but that they should put themselves in the Body and let the whole Body do the work.

THE APPOINTMENT OF THE RESPONSIBLE ONES
OF THE LOCAL CHURCH

First Helping Them Learn to Bear Responsibility

Certain brothers asked: If we appoint some brothers to be the responsible ones of a local church, there is still some question concerning whether or not they are fit to be elders. But if we do not appoint them, the church is paralyzed. What shall we do?

Answer: You can ask the few brothers whom you feel are promising and let them first learn to bear responsibility. You need to guide them to bear responsibility.

Being Difficult to Change

I think there is one aspect that we should pay attention to when we guide them to bear responsibility. It is spoken of in the Epistle to Timothy that some become deacons first and then elders. Therefore, you need to speak to them in a careful way. Let them know that you are preparing to ask them to be deacons. Do not tell them immediately that you may be choosing them to be elders. First, see whether or not they can be deacons. In this way you can see who particularly grows in the Lord. After a period of time, perhaps two or three months, you can place them in the office of the eldership or of a deacon. If you first appoint them as elders and change afterwards, it will be very difficult. To make a change with a deacon is still a relatively easy matter, but to make a change with an elder is not easy at all.

Considering the Spiritual Future

Therefore, especially in selecting the elders, your eyes must be wide open. Consider what their spiritual future will be. This does not mean that we cannot make mistakes. We are prone to make mistakes. The issue is spiritual; therefore, you need to be very careful before God, and lead these brothers into this realm. If you see that an elder is unfit and replace him at any time, you cause wounds. It is awkward if you set up the authority and then overthrow it later. Therefore, learn to pay attention before God to the spiritual condition of those brothers and their spiritual future.

Many people are good material. Do not damage them, but guide them properly and cause them to learn to bear responsibility year after year. After some time you can ask them to bear responsibility formally when you go into their midst. We should not be in a hurry to say that we are setting up elders. Whether or not we have the assurance, we should tell them, "Come, and I will help you, the more promising brothers, learn how to take care of the affairs of the church." Demonstrate to them. To some brothers we may say, "You can be a responsible brother," and to some others we may say, "You can be a deacon." But be careful. Do not first ask him to be an elder and later ask him to be a deacon. This would be difficult. If a person is humble, it would not do much damage, but once human feeling comes in, it is a very difficult situation.

HELPING THE RESPONSIBLE BROTHERS
IN THE SURROUNDING AREAS

In the future you can do a very profitable thing in a local church which is also the center of the work. For example, if you are in Peking and you see that there are three very good brothers in Sui-Yuan and another two very good brothers in T'ai-yuan, you can invite them to come to Peking. The meeting of the responsible brothers in Peking should be open to them.

This meeting is not open to everyone. It should not be open to sisters. We do not allow sisters to attend. Today if a brother comes from T'ai-yuan and attends this meeting, it is a very great privilege we extend to him. We may tell him, "This meeting is not for others, and we do not lightly open the door to anyone. Today we invite you to come and live here for a month or two with the hope that you can learn something."

At the beginning let him sit in the meeting, without saying anything. He should learn to observe how you manage spiritual things before God, how problems are solved, how questions are raised and discussed, how prayers are offered, how to sense before God whether or not a certain thing should be done, and how to make a decision when peace is obtained. Then show him how to answer the questions the brothers and sisters bring, how you fellowship with brothers from out of town, how you receive those who ask to participate in the breaking of bread, and how you fellowship with those who want to be baptized. Present a pattern to him. After a period of time, you can say to him, "Please speak to this brother on our behalf." Then you should observe how he speaks.

After some time, perhaps you may send him back. Let him do the work of an overseer in T'ai-yuan without giving him the name. A little later, you might go to T'ai-yuan and hear what the saints there are saying. Not all the criticisms will be correct, but you need to know the things this brother has done. The criticisms of some brothers are not correct because they do not submit to authority. If this brother is actually wrong, you have to see where the problem is. When you go to visit the second time, you should be clear whether or not that brother can bear the responsibility.

For this reason it is necessary to have strong meetings at the center of the work, where the apostles are. You need to help the meetings of the overseers so that you will be able to help the responsible brothers in this district through this church. Otherwise, you have no way to help them because you do not have any pattern to show them. You have no pathway to lead them on.

For a brother who has the qualification before the Lord and who can learn to be a responsible brother, you should let him learn in the center of the work through the meeting. Then his eyes will be opened to realize that he has been reckless in his own locality. Many times brothers have told me that they now realize what they did in the church before was really reckless. Many people have never seen what a spiritual church is and how a spiritual church should be taken care of. Many times they just come together and make decisions in a light way.

In the meeting you should hold the rein and also let the responsible brothers in that locality hold the rein. Show them that this meeting is more serious than the time Moses was on the mountain. He was only given the law, but we are taking care of the church. To take care of the church is more serious than Moses going up to the mountain to receive two tablets of stone. Therefore, you should make your home in the church where the center of the work is. That place must be strong. Only when it is strong do you have the way to make the churches in the surrounding area strong and bring them into the presence of the Lord.

THINGS TO PAY ATTENTION TO
IN THE MEETING OF THE OVERSEERS

Being Solemn

In the meeting of the overseers, you need to bring in all solemnity. There should not be joking and light conversation. When you come into this meeting, you should say, "We are handling things before God and should not have a loose attitude." This is the time the High Priest enters into the Holiest, and this is the time we come before God to serve Him. Here there is no joking. We come before God to see how the work in this area should be. Unnecessary words should be reduced, for if they abound, two or three hours will slip away and all your time will be gone. Everybody should come together in a serious way and consider things item by item.

Not Talking behind Others' Backs

If there is any responsible brother who comes to the meeting of the overseers and does not give his opinion in the meeting, but gives it in front of the brothers and sisters, you should rebuke him before the brothers in the next meeting: "You are not qualified to be a responsible brother!" If you have a feeling or something to say, you should bring it up in the meeting of the overseers when all the brothers are together. If someone does not speak in the meeting of the overseers, yet goes out and speaks to others, he is a person with a double tongue. Such a person cannot be in our midst. You must rebuke him sharply, saying, "Brother, this is not the way a Christian behaves, nor is it becoming to a saint. We should not do such a thing. In the meeting of the overseers, if you have some feeling before God, you should open your mouth. If you do not open your mouth here, you should not open your mouth to speak in any other place."

Please remember that the life of the whole church in the early phase is in the meeting of the overseers. If you cause the meeting of the overseers to become light, loose, or sloppy and if decisions are based merely on some conversation without any prayer, the work in that area is over and useless. In that place there will be no spiritual weight at all. If you have nothing in your storehouse, what resources are you going to spread to other places? This meeting must be strong. There are requirements for the responsible brothers coming to this meeting: If any word is not worth mentioning in this place, it is not worth mentioning in any other place. If they want to open their mouths, they should open their mouths in this place. If they do not open their mouths in this place, they should not open their mouths in any other place.

I hope that the responsible brothers in all the localities know that if any brother goes out of the meeting of the overseers and speaks a word behind the other brothers' backs, he has to bear full responsibility before God. No human emotion should enter in, and by no means can we be loose in this matter. We must charge strictly: "Brother, this is not Christian behavior." We must speak to him in front of all: "If you have anything to bring up, you must bring it up in front of the responsible ones among the co-workers; if you bring it up behind their back to any other person, you damage the oneness of the Body."

Not Telling the Wives

There is another matter. No one can go home and tell his wife anything that takes place in the meeting of the overseers. Nor can any brother go out and tell a second brother anything that happens in the meeting of the overseers. This is something divine, and everyone should maintain it. In this meeting the same principles apply in everything; you cannot speak lightly, you cannot leak out information, and you should not have unnecessary words. Therefore, I hope that you will be strict concerning this matter. Do not be loose. Train the brothers, especially the responsible brothers, and let them realize how to handle things before God. Do not let them be careless. Whenever things are handled before God, they must be done seriously. Unless all agree that certain matters can be made public, they should not be told to others. There is no need to be told every time that you cannot tell anyone. Not telling others is the principle. The things in the meeting of the overseers should not be passed on to others.

Not Mentioning How Decisions Were Made

If there are things which should be made public, the responsible brothers should go out and tell the brothers. But as to how this matter was decided and handled in the meeting of the overseers, it is better that these words be buried in the grave. You need not tell how the decision was made. This is a matter before God, not a matter to be talked about. I hope that the brothers will learn to pay attention to these things.

THE IMPORTANCE OF THE MEETING OF THE OVERSEERS

All the Meetings Being Uplifted

If this meeting is strong before God, all the other meetings will spontaneously be uplifted. This meeting is the center of everything. If this meeting is high, all the meetings during the week will be uplifted.

Concentrating One's Entire Being in This Meeting

Taking care of a meeting of the overseers requires a great deal of spiritual strength. You should concentrate your entire being, and the brothers who are with you should do the same. Then you can consider things item by item.

The Watchtower of the Church

This meeting is the watchtower of the whole church. The saints are not aware of many things, but you know them first. The saints have not seen many things, but you see them first. The saints have no feeling many times, but you have some feeling first. It is in this meeting that everything is sensed first. Before the difficulties around you are apparent, you can sense them in this meeting. Therefore, many times when things happen, you have anticipated the situation and taken care of it already. As time goes on, your eyes should become keener and keener. You need to learn to use your eyes to look ahead to the things in the future. With more time your sense should become keener and keener, and you will be able to know what will happen and what will not happen.

I am not saying that there should be no prayer and no waiting on the Lord in your personal time, but I am saying that the overseers' meeting is the time for corporate dealing, and you should prepare for this meeting in your private time. If you do not prepare in your private time, when you come to the overseers' meeting, you will have nothing to say; when you come each time, nothing will happen. Do you see this? If there is nothing happening in the overseers' meeting, it is an evidence, a proof, that every brother is lazy before God, that even all the responsible brothers are corporately lazy before Him. If a few responsible brothers are strong before God, their eyes will be open, they will watch and observe, and spontaneously many things will be going on with them. The High Priest bore the breastplate of the twelve tribes of Israel, and he bore it all the time. This means that he could not take it off. You should learn to bear the breastplate every day, and then you will discover something concerning God's people every day. Not one of our overseers' meetings has enough time. You may feel that three or four hours or five or six hours have passed by very quickly. Sometimes in the meeting of the overseers you need to cut your words short because there is no more time.

Once the meeting of the overseers is strong, it will be easy for other things in the church life to be strong, because in the meeting of the overseers you can have much consideration about all the meetings. If the gospel meeting has become weak, we need to concentrate all our strength there, and the saints need to do likewise. The meeting of the overseers is the watchtower of the church, the place to keep the watch.

Being Respected by All the Brothers

You need to continue working until one day all the brothers

and sisters respect the meeting of the overseers. They will know that this day or this half a day is the time the responsible brothers go before God to take care of things. I often think that the meeting of the overseers is like the prayer room of John G. Paton's father. I often feel that in the whole world there was not another father like him. That old father may not have been aware of what happened, but his few sons all knew. His house was not very large. On one side was a room, on the other side was a kitchen, and in the middle there was a little study. When the door of this little study was shut, all the sons knew that their father had gone before God to deal with things. At such a time, no child dared to make a noise, and everyone walked softly. They could not forget the sighings they heard from inside that room even forty or fifty years afterwards. Paton himself said, "Even today I can still hear my father interceding for me in that room." He knew that this was a serious matter. Therefore, we should also let all the saints know that the day the responsible brothers deal with things before God is a designated day. Some brothers have given their all to go before God on behalf of the church.

Thus, you will see something issue out from the church; the church will have a way. Therefore, the matter of the overseers' meeting is upon the shoulders of you responsible brothers. Let me say again that you need to start from the center of the work in this region. Do a strong, absolute, and serious work. Afterward, you can invite the brothers from out of town.

Two Different Aspects

Before God we need two different aspects. First, we need the fellowship of the brothers and sisters. After paying attention to this matter in our midst for twenty years, I think that we are gradually making progress. It was different twenty years ago. Thank God that today this situation has had a great change. Today, at least, the saints have feelings toward one another.

Second, we need to know God's authority. Brotherly love is one thing, and being a servant before God is something else. You need to take orders. If we want to go out to work, before we go we need to hear the word before God. We need to learn these things together in these days.

The Most Solemn Time

We need to know that no hour is more solemn than this hour. This is the most solemn time. Learn to look to the Lord in a single way. We need to know what to do before God. We need to be confident, godly, single for service, and without any barrier between us and the Lord. We should do all things well in every aspect. Then we will have a clear pathway ahead of us.

In all other times, we may be intimate with one another. However, when we come to this meeting, it is not a matter of how well we know each other, for this is the time we truly go before God. In ordinary times we talk about brotherly love. At this time we do not talk about brotherly love. This is the time for us to go to God together to be His servants. We are before God to receive directions together to go out to work. Learn to solemnly hear God's word before Him.

When we do not know God's will, we need to say so, and we should ask, search, learn, and pray before God.

When our condition is right and the brothers come together, it will be a simple matter without much difficulty. It is a serious matter for us to go before God.

The Question of Number

I also want to bring up the matter of number. If there are five, six, seven, or eight co-workers who can coordinate together, then the meeting of the overseers can have twenty to thirty people. There is no need to have more. If there are more, the meeting will be hard to handle. We need to set a number for the meeting that we can handle. If we can manage three, bring in three. If we can manage ten, bring in ten. Do not bring in more people than we can manage. Learn to know that we are before God as if we were conducting a military council. This has to be very strict.

We may let those who come to learn from out of town go back after two or three months and do their work properly.

I believe that one day all of God's children will gradually realize that at least once a week a group of brothers go before God to deal with things on their behalf and on behalf of the whole church.

CHAPTER TWO

THE PRIESTLY SERVICE

We should first establish the principle that all of God's children are priests who should serve God. With this principle in view, let us see how we can lead all the brothers and sisters to be priests in a local church. In other words what kind of arrangement should we have in the spiritual work so that all the believers can participate in the spiritual things, both the new believers and those who have known the Lord for many years? We need to see which spiritual things in a local church can be taken care of by the brothers and sisters.

A FEW SPIRITUAL MATTERS
THAT ALL THE BELIEVERS SHOULD DO

In the beginning in Foochow and also in Shanghai, we arranged a few matters which were to be done by all the local brothers and sisters. First, there is the preaching of the gospel.

Second, after a person has heard the gospel and received the Lord, we should go to visit him, bringing him into the right way and showing him how to become a Christian.

Third, there is the visitation of new believers. How should we render help to those who have come from other religions, have believed in the Lord, have come to the right way, and have been baptized?

Fourth, in the church there are still many other needs. Some believers have difficulties in their families; some have sicknesses; some suffer in poverty; some have funerals or other special occasions in their families. There are all these kinds of situations among God's children. These people also need the service and help of the church. We can categorize such services as the visitation of those in special situations.

This is another thing which all the brothers and sisters can do.

Fifth, there is the care for the brothers and sisters who have moved away and for those who have moved from other places. I have always felt that this is a very important matter. If brothers and sisters move away to other cities, even though they have a letter of recommendation, we should still take care of them afterwards. We also need to take special care of those brothers and sisters who have come from other places.

These five items are sufficient for our consideration of spiritual matters.

Preaching the Gospel

The first thing we need to pay attention to is that among the ministers of the word established by God in the church, one is called an evangelist. However, Paul told Timothy that he should do the work of an evangelist (2 Tim. 4:5). When we compare these two, we see a very important matter, that is, God has established a category of people in the church called evangelists; but to those who are not evangelists, the command of the apostle is that they should do the work of an evangelist. In other words, those who are evangelists should preach the gospel, and those who are not evangelists should do the work of an evangelist. An evangelist is a gift specifically established by God. If God has given you the gift to be an evangelist, then you should concentrate on preaching the gospel to bring people into the church. However, if you are not established by God as an evangelist, the Lord's word is that all of God's children should do the work of an evangelist.

In other words, concerning the work of preaching the gospel, he who can do it should do it, and he who cannot do it should also do it. The evangelist, who is one who can do it, has to do it. Those who are not evangelists, that is, the ones who cannot do it, should do it also. This work should be everywhere. Young ones such as Timothy should do it. In fact everyone in every place should do the work of an evangelist.

For this we have to encourage all the brothers and sisters to spend time going out to do the work of preaching the gospel. We should never allow them to be lazy and forget about sinners and should never allow just a few to do the work of preaching the gospel. It should be made known to all the brothers and sisters that everyone is a priest and that everyone should serve God. There is a service that is called the service of the gospel. In spiritual work and spiritual service, there is one item called the work of an evangelist. We must help the brothers to pay special attention to this point.

Caring for the Gospel

Caring for the gospel is something that we should practice before God. I hope that all the brothers and sisters can bear the responsibility of caring for sinners in the work of preaching the gospel.

This responsibility starts with bringing a person to the meetings until he is baptized. You need to show the brothers and sisters how great their responsibility is in bringing a person from home, from school, from a hospital, or from an office to the meetings. They should keep bringing him until he has been led to know the Lord, has received the Lord, and has been baptized. This is what should be done in the care and visitation of the gospel.

Bringing People to the Gospel Meetings

When you take care of a sinner, you have to find a way to bring him to the gospel meeting. One should not bring too many at one time. Of course, if you bring many, it is also good. But if you want them to be well taken care of, it would be better for one person to bring only three or four. If you bring too many, then you will not be able to take care of them. We do not want to set up a law, but two to four is a good number. Do not bring too many; but this is not to say that if opportunity allows, you cannot bring more. If you can bring thirty or fifty students from school, that is good too. But when you do, you need to immediately ask the responsible brothers to help you find some brothers or sisters who can share the responsibility of taking care of them. Suppose you can take care of only four persons, but you have brought forty.

There are still thirty-six whom you are unable to take care of. Therefore, you need to ask the responsible brothers to make arrangements for a few brothers and sisters to help care for them.

Sitting between Them

Now we must see the way of taking care of the gospel meeting. You have to prepare Bibles and hymnals. You should arrange the four new ones so that two sit on your left and two on your right. No more than two should be on one side. Any more than that would make caring for them inconvenient. When the Bible is read, you need to help them find the verses. When hymns are sung, you need to help them find the hymns. To many, you need to explain the way the pages are laid out. If the chorus of a hymn needs to be sung each time, you need to tell them this as well. You should not consider that everyone is so capable. They may have never sung a hymn or read the Bible before, so you need to help them.

During the time of preaching, if someone does not understand, you need to explain to him in a soft voice. Do you remember the story Mr. Wakes once told while he was preaching in Shanghai? He said that once a British preacher went to Japan and was preaching in a very large public area on a day when many people were there. The preacher's first words were, "You all know how the Israelites went out of Egypt." When Mr. Wakes heard this, he immediately ran up to tell him that he might need to spend two hours to explain who the Israelites were and what it meant to go out of Egypt. We have to realize that there are many things that people do not understand. Although we may not be able to spend two hours to explain as Mr. Wakes suggested, we can at least use a couple of sentences to explain to them in our softest voice.

Strengthening with Prayer
the Word Being Preached

Your greatest job is to help the preaching in the meeting. The preaching of the gospel is not for you to hear, nor is it for you to criticize. The preaching from the podium is for sinners to hear. Many times the gospel has not been preached well, because the brothers did not listen properly. Keep in mind that you are not there to criticize, but to help. The gospel is not being preached for you to hear; the gospel is being preached for sinners to hear. Therefore, when you realize that some weighty words are being spoken or that some words are being spoken with a released spirit, you need to pray quietly while sitting next to them. You may pray, "O Lord, impart this word into the people!" or "O Lord, use this word to save this person!" or "O Lord, use this word to save these two!" It may be that the Lord will give you two because you asked for two. If you say one, the Lord will give you one. If you say five, the Lord will give you five. You strengthen the word being preached with your prayer for the four who are under your care. As you are taking care of them, you are praying. This is what you should do in the meeting, and this is something everyone should be responsible for.

Willing to Be Assigned to Attend to the New Ones

Those who did not bring anyone should take care of the surplus brought by others. During the gospel preaching, all these brothers should sit aside and wait to be assigned by the brother who is responsible for handling the care of new ones that day. Listening to the gospel requires companionship. They listen to the gospel and you attend to them. You need to sit next to these new ones, perhaps two or four of them, to listen with them, even though you did not bring them.

During the preaching, the brothers and sisters should either stand by the door or, if space allows, sit at the back of the meeting to wait to be assigned by the brother who is responsible for handling the care of the new ones that day. If you see several new people come in, you should go and sit next to them to help them. Caring for the gospel has two aspects. On the one hand, we need to bring people, and on the other hand, we need to take care of them in the meetings. Everyone should bring people and take care of those whom he brings. Those who have not brought anyone should also learn to take care of the people that others have brought to the meeting. All the brothers and sisters have to be brought to the point where they all have something to do.

While the Net Is Being Drawn

Whenever we preach the gospel, we must always draw the net. To cast the net is one thing, and to draw the net is another. You are not asking the fish to jump into the net; you are drawing the net. When the preaching is over and the one at the podium begins to draw the net by exhorting people to raise their hands to indicate their willingness to receive the gospel, you need to help in this work. It does not matter what method he uses. Some may use one method, and others may use another method. None of these things matter. These things are flexible. As long as he can draw the net, even if he has to jump into the ocean to do it, it will be all right. At this time you need to help him do the work of drawing the net. You also have to help the ones who have been brought. Among those you care for, you will have much to do. On the one hand, you need to pray, and on the other hand, you need to be quite strong to persuade them, saying, "I think you should stand up to receive the Lord due to your sin." If you have the assurance that pride has hindered them from standing up, you could say, "You should be humble. You should not be proud. You should receive the Lord." Or if you know that the love of the world is the reason that they will not stand up, you could say, "Is there anything in the world worth your lingering? Why should you wait for another time? If you feel that the time is ripe, do not wait."

Not Waiting for Four Months

The most important thing in gospel preaching is not to wait for four months. Many people make a common mistake of waiting for four months. But the Lord Jesus told us not to wait for four months. The word of the Lord Jesus was very peculiar. He said, "Do you not say that there are yet four months and then the harvest comes? Behold, I tell you,...they are already white for harvest" (John 4:35). Two or three days may be all right, but four months is too long. The harvest of the gospel goes far beyond man's concept. Do not be so foolish as to think that you still have to wait four months after the seeds are sown. The Lord Jesus said that if you sow the seeds today, you can harvest today. There is not such a principle of waiting for four months.

As the gospel is being preached while you are sitting next to people, according to your feeling the time may or may not be ripe. However, you should not be limited by the time factor. If the person is ripe, you need to encourage him to believe; if he is not ripe, you still need to encourage him to believe. There is absolutely no such principle of waiting for four months. You may not expect someone to believe, but when he believes, he believes. You may consider another to be ripe, but it turns out that he is absolutely unreliable. Therefore, you must encourage all to believe.

Some people seem to be completely ignorant. But please remember that whether or not someone can understand does not depend upon you; it depends upon whether or not the Holy Spirit shines on him. I know at least several brothers who first believed in a false way but who were eventually saved in a genuine way. They were forced by others to believe, but eventually they genuinely believed. Therefore, as far as encouraging others to believe, you should not decide before-hand how you will do it. Sometimes the opportunity is ripe, so you need to encourage them; at other times the opportunity is not ripe, but you still need to encourage them.

After the Meeting

After the meeting is over, you should stay with them to lead them to pray and to talk with them. You should always bring them before the Lord, lead them to pray and receive Him, and then help them record their names. When recording their names, you need to make sure the street address and the house number are correct. In the past many report slips had wrong house numbers, so a great deal of effort was wasted when we tried to visit them later. If possible, add a question such as, "When are you most free?" or "When is the most convenient time for you?" When you record their names, you should write them down quickly so that the new ones will not be annoyed by your slow writing. After the report slips are completed, you have to turn them in to the responsible brothers. Afterward, other brothers can visit them to share more with them.

Imparting the Need, the Knowledge, and the Decisiveness into People

Some people receive the Lord because they have a need, but they do not have the knowledge of the gospel. Others have the knowledge of the gospel, but they do not have a need. Still others feel that they have a need and also the knowledge, but they cannot make the decision at that very moment. All these are matters that you need to work on. To those who do not have a need, you have to impart the need. To those who do not have the knowledge, you have to impart the knowledge. To those who lack decisiveness, you have to impart decisiveness.

Telling Them about Baptism

After you have brought them to the point where they are quite clear, you need to immediately tell them about baptism. You have to visit them once, twice, or three times; how many times, we do not know. When you get to the point that they can be baptized, you should then turn them over to the responsible brothers.

Before the Meeting Starts

Another matter presents a very difficult problem when attending a gospel meeting. Before the meeting starts, we see five or ten rows of people just sitting there. Some might have come one hour early. There are two places in which the passage of time is particularly long: one is hell and the other is the church meeting. When a person goes to hell, he feels that the time there is very long. When an unsaved person comes to a church meeting, he also feels that the time there is very long. He is not saved and he feels that the time is long. He may come quite a while before the preaching of the gospel starts. If he leaves, he does not feel right, and if he just sits there, he feels like he is in a fog. This hour of waiting is very unbearable. Sometimes I do have a deep feeling concerning this matter. I saw some who brought new ones to the meeting and had them sit there row by row, waiting for some period of time. Some had to wait for half an hour, some an hour. If you looked at their faces, they were just like those whom the Lord Jesus saw, who were "cast away like sheep not having a shepherd" (Matt. 9:36). What do you expect them to do? If you ask them to go home and come back again, there is not enough time. If you have them sit there and wait, they have nothing to do. Therefore, before the meeting starts, you also need to take care of them.

Never allow the unbelievers to sit together by themselves. From the very beginning you should always seat two or four of them next to one believer. The ones who do this work must be equipped with full armor by having tracts, printed gospel messages, and Bibles ready for the literate to read, and they have to talk to those who cannot read well or are illiterate. In any case all the brothers and sisters should be there taking care of them. If you let them sit there without anything to do, they will become cold even if they were like hot water at the beginning. Therefore, you have to learn to sit among them.

All Becoming Priests

There is no way for this work to be done without everyone serving. You need to show the brothers and sisters that everyone is a priest; hence, everyone should have things to do. If this is the case, immediately you will see that all the gospel meetings in every place will be quite prevailing. This is the church preaching the gospel. We must pay special attention to this word. It is the church that is preaching the gospel. All the brothers and sisters are working; they all are priests and they all have come to serve. If this is not the case, there is no church. So do not boast that you have the local church in such and such a place. Where is the church today?

The Number of Priests Determining
the Number of God's People

Let me repeat something that I have said for many years. I have a particularly deep feeling about this today. The number of people serving determines the number of people in the church. In a locality the number in the church is the number of people serving. The number of priests determines the number of God's people. You should not turn it around and say that the number of God's people determines the number of priests. This is wrong. The number of priests determines the number of God's people. The number of serving ones determines the number of God's people.

No Useless Members

When I was in England, I met a brother who was very knowledgeable. He said that there were many members with a function and there were also many members without a function. But I said that in the Bible all the members have a function and that there are no members without a function. If there is a member without a function, it is probably the appendix. When he heard that, he laughed. Many people think that some members have a function and that other members do not. Can you tell me which member does not have a function? Where is the member that does not have a function? In the whole body the only member without a function is the appendix, and you should not consider that it refers to you by coincidence. The appendix is the member of the body which is most frequently removed. Please remember that all the members have a function. May we see today that the number of members with a function is the number of members in the Body.

A Body of Priests

We have to change our way of thinking. Today we must see that serving means that the whole church serves and preaching the gospel means that the whole church preaches the gospel. To serve as priests involves everyone. The number of brothers and sisters serving determines the number of members in a locality. The number of people serving determines the number of brothers and sisters in the church. We should always determine the number of brothers and sisters in the church based upon the number of serving ones. Hence, there should not be one thousand or five thousand brothers in a locality and only a few serving. Among us we cannot tolerate any members being functionless. We cannot have even one member without a function. Please remember that as a member of the Body of Christ, you have a function. It is impossible for you not to have a function. If you do not see this basic principle, you will not do the work well. Brothers and sisters, frankly speaking, you cannot do the work. That is not the New Testament; that is deformed Catholicism with the system of priests. We do not have a system of priests; rather, we are a body of priests. Everyone is a priest.

Caring for New Believers

The Meeting for Edifying New Believers

After a person has believed, is baptized, and becomes a new believer, we should bring him to our prearranged meeting for edifying new believers. In this meeting we will have a special topic for them to get into every week.

Making Up Lessons and Rendering the Care

Once a person has started coming to the meeting for edifying new believers, he should be placed under the care of those believers in the church who are more mature than he. How should this care be rendered? Those who take care of the new believers must make sure that the new believers are practicing the lessons presented every week.

If they do not come to a meeting, you must immediately visit them and give them a make-up lesson. Of those who come to the meetings, during the week you must seek out the five or ten under your care and see whether they understand the lesson that was shared that week.

At this point I want to have a little fellowship with you brothers, especially with those who are ministers of the word. I think that we all have had many experiences which may have been heartbreaking, shameful, and embarrassing, and even some experiences which made us angry. Today you may have shared a message that was quite high, but if you check with the brothers, the message was like a wind passing over the rooftop. There was not even a breeze next to their ears or even above their heads. If you do not believe it, just ask them to raise questions after your speaking and see what kind of questions they have. I have always said that the questions asked reveal how the listeners are doing; the preaching reveals how the preacher is doing. After a most spiritual message is presented and the listeners are given opportunity to ask questions, you often see that they have veered off considerably, even to the extent that it is beyond what you could imagine.

Therefore, we should not think that the new believers will understand simply because the message was spoken from the podium. You need to go and visit these new believers. This is the visitation of the new believers or the care for the new believers. You have to make the message up for anyone who has not heard it, and you have to see how it was received by anyone who did hear it. They do not have it simply by hearing the sound or by counting the number of times per second my voice vibrates in the air. We want them to hear clearly the words of the lesson. Therefore, concerning this matter, the brothers responsible for the care of the new believers need to labor in a careful way.

Having the New Believers
Care for the Unbelievers

Another aspect we need to pay attention to is that all the new believers can immediately take care of the unbelievers. However, we should place a few strong brothers to work together with them. A brother who has been saved for a number of years should coordinate with them and take care of them by leading them step by step. You have to show the new believers that as they have already believed in the Lord, they are priests before Him. All the priests must have a service. Today this service before God is to serve either the unbelievers or the new believers. How well the new believers do in this matter depends altogether on how well you take care of them.

Laboring on the Fifty-two Topics

Everyone knows now that fifty-two topics have been

prepared for edifying the new believers each year. From these fifty-two topics we will prepare one topic each week to speak on. The older brothers need to be very familiar with these topics and should practice them themselves. After they have practiced them, they have to lead the new believers to practice also. Furthermore, they have to become very familiar with the new believers because many of these fifty-two topics stress the matter of conduct, and therefore they require concentrated effort to apply them. After they have done it themselves, they can know the real situation with the new brothers so that they can encourage or even urge them to do it also. This is not something we can take care of merely by listening to messages. Just listening to messages will not suffice; there needs to be the practice. We need to reach the point where we can say, "I have to practice it myself." Therefore, on the one hand, you have to preach this message to them, and on the other hand, there must be brothers who will make the effort to deal with them concerning the particular topic each week. Go and seek them out, urge them, make them decide, and make them practice. With many problems, it is not a matter of just one visitation, but a matter of caring for them for several weeks or months. With the matter of reading the Bible and prayer, you have to see whether in fact they have read the Bible in an adequate way, and whether they have progressed in their prayer. The church needs to lay great stress on these matters before she can be brought to a proper condition. Therefore, I hope that we, especially the co-workers, would see that it is for this reason that I stressed that the problem today is not a matter of knowledge but a matter of taking the lead. All the local churches need to do this wholeheartedly. Since this work is so heavy, we cannot let it pass by carelessly.

Being a Master Builder

The way we are taking today is absolutely different from our way in the past. Today the workers should not do the work, but the workers should cause others to do the work. Is this clear? If the workers are always working by themselves, this matter can never be done well. I say again that if you go out to work and only you yourselves are working, you have failed. Paul not only worked by himself; he was also a master builder. You need to learn to work, and you also need to learn to be a master builder who leads other brothers and sisters to work. This is the way we should work with the unbelievers as well as with the new believers.

There are enough things to keep you busy just with the new believers alone. You have to learn before God how to lead many brothers one by one to give make-up lessons to these new believers. These brothers should go one by one to the homes of the new believers and examine how well they are practicing the lessons. They should check carefully one by one whether or not the lesson was practiced that week. The brothers should exhort the new believers to read the Bible every day and should check to see if they have read it the day they visit them. It is not a matter of whether or not the message was spoken; it is a matter of whether or not, having heard the word, the new believers have practiced it. The brothers must suggest that they use a prayer notebook. They then need to go and check how their prayer has been and whether or not they have written names in their notebook. One brother may have written down five names and another may have written down five thousand names. What should the brothers do? Is the one with five names right or is the one with five thousand names right? The brothers should advise them that they should not write down five thousand names; that is too many. You have to arrange things one by one and show them how things are arranged.

Caring for Problems

In caring for problems there is no need for too many brothers to be involved. The work of preaching the gospel, caring for the gospel, and caring for the new believers requires the mobilization of almost everyone. Caring for problems, however, should not be carried out in this way. There are brothers and sisters who have a spiritual measure before the Lord which is weightier than that of others, and it should be quite weighty. There need not be too many of this kind of brothers. Not more than four or five of these brothers are necessary to address a particular need. If a brother has encountered hardship, these brothers then need to help him. If there are some who have joyous occasions, these brothers should rejoice with them, help them, and pray with them. If there are some who are sorrowful over a death, these brothers should be sorrowful together with them, helping them and praying together with them. There may be some who have difficulties and conflicts in their family; these brothers need to resolve the problems for them, pray for them, and comfort them. Problem matters such as these or matters such as helping the poor can all be given to the brothers and sisters responsible for taking care of problems.

In the church, when brothers encounter problems, or if some special situations arise, you need to allow these brothers and sisters to make some arrangements concerning these problems among the saints. Whenever brothers and sisters hear that something has happened among some of the brothers and sisters, they need to immediately notify these brothers and sisters and allow them to find a way to meet the need. Send money to those in poverty; feed those who are hungry; clothe those who have nothing to wear; comfort those with difficulties; visit those who are in prison; pray for those who are sick; solve the problems of those who have family difficulties.

A Foolish Thought

I want the brothers and sisters to know about a foolish thought. I do not know when this thought began. Some people indeed have the thought that in the church life we should not encounter problems. But please remember that problems have existed from the time of the apostolic church. Since the time of the apostolic church, the church has always been a church of problems, not a church without problems. You should never consider that a situation in which there are many problems implies an inadequate condition of the church. Please remember that not many days after the day of Pentecost, the problem of Ananias and Sapphira occurred in the church, and not many days after that, the problem of the Grecian widows happened. Later, Stephen was martyred, and Peter was thrown into prison. These kinds of things continued to happen. The history of the church since the beginning is one that is full of problems. Only a worldly church will have few problems; the genuine church always has many problems. I do not know the source of this foolish thought. There is not one church that is always serene, without any difficulties or failures. There has always been blessing on the one hand and difficulties on the other hand.

At the time of the apostles, the church had the most difficulties. Look at the seven churches in Revelation. The five that were damaged had little persecution. One church, the church in Smyrna, was not rebuked by the Lord, but Smyrna was a church that suffered martyrdom. One church, the church in Philadelphia, was praised by God. The Lord said to that church, "You have kept the word of My endurance" (3:10). There were many things that required the church there to endure. To keep the Lord's word is not to keep the Lord's word of tranquillity, but the Lord's word of endurance. There were many things the church had to pass through. You should never think that if the church is peaceful and tranquil, going on steadily, then this is the unique proof of the Lord's blessing. The church may have many problems, but that does not mean that the Lord is not blessing. Therefore, the brothers responsible for caring for problems have to make arrangements to handle all the difficulties in the church.

Caring for the Believers Who Have Moved Away and for Those from Other Places

The last item related to spiritual affairs is the care for the brothers and sisters who have moved away and for the brothers and sisters who have come from other places.

Regarding Brothers Who Move Away

Writing a Letter of Recommendation Not Being the Last Responsibility

After a brother moves away, the writing of a letter of recommendation should never be the last responsibility, as is the situation today, where once a brother moves away, we simply write the letter and everything is over. How is it going with him since he moved away? How is the church where he is? We do not know. This may be how the brother is lost. The brothers in Foochow have suffered in this way. Only letters of recommendation were written, and this is how some were lost. This clearly is a failure of the work of a local church.

The Need for Some to Be Responsible for Correspondence

I hope that when there is a brother or a sister who moves away from your locality, there would be a number of brothers who would do two things with them. Some must be responsible to correspond with them and inform them of the situation in their former church. This should be something definite. When a brother moves away, we need to investigate who in the meetings was especially close to him and whether anyone corresponds with him. For a long time in Shanghai I felt ashamed, even to the point of condemnation, that one person moved away and no one corresponded with him for five years. That was the end of him. We do not even know the situation with him. We are really ashamed. I thought that there must have been brothers who were corresponding with him. But, as it turned out, no one was corresponding with him, and that was the end of him.

Some people have moved to the villages and have become lost. We would need to spend much labor to recover them. We cannot continue to lose people and at the same time preach the gospel. This is not profitable.

Whenever a brother moves away, there should be some brothers who are assigned to correspond with him. We should write him either one letter a week or two letters a month, but no less than one letter a month. We should always correspond with him by letter to inform him of the situation in the meetings and of the situation of the brothers and sisters. We cannot be loose about this kind of situation. If there were ten letters of recommendation written today, these should be brought to the responsible brothers, who should tell two or three other brothers that a brother has now moved to Peking or Amoy. They should say, "We would like you to write him at least one letter a month. Whether or not you are busy, you need to correspond with him." This is a service. In our correspondence, we should not write vain things nor should we write in a loose way. We should specifically mention what the situation is among the brothers in the meetings and their spiritual condition.

For each person moving away, there should be at least a few who correspond with him. Or two can be assigned specifically to be responsible for all these ones. They have to be responsible for taking care of the brothers who have moved away. They need to find out regularly if the ones who moved away have corresponded in return and whether they have encountered difficulties; they need to find out how they are doing.

If we work in this way, God will bless us. Every one of these brothers who has moved away will be accounted for, and each one of them will be able to stand firm. We have to labor on this matter attentively. This is something we have learned after suffering for many years. We have lost many people in this way. Therefore, I hope the brothers from every locality will be quite strict in this matter. When a brother among us moves away, we always need to tie a string to him as if he were a kite. A string should always be in our hand. There should always be two or three brothers who have fellowship with him. If this is the case, the problems will be greatly reduced. If he has some special situations in the other place, we can notify the brothers in his locality. There will always be a way to take care of him; otherwise, we will lose him. Then there will be nothing more that we can do.

Sending Him Excerpts

When there are special messages in the meetings or when there is a good word in the preaching of the gospel, some brothers need to record them. They should record the central point of the message. They do not need to write down everything, nor do they need to record all the messages given in a particular month. They need to write down only the important and central points. At the very least, this can be a supply to the brothers who are absent from the meetings.

Suppose a brother moves from Foochow to Shanghai. Never consider that since you have already written a letter of recommendation, you have washed your hands of the matter. If you do this, after recommending the person, you will not know whether or not the other side has received him. You will not know where he lives and what his situation is, and you will not know the situation of the church there. Therefore, on the one hand, there is the need among us for several brothers to correspond with him; on the other hand, some brothers need to be responsible to record the words spoken in the meetings, whether they are words spoken to believers or words of the gospel, and send them to that brother at least once a month. They can be sent in a letter or as a printed copy. You can tell him that in a meeting a certain brother gave a very good illustration or that in a meeting a certain brother spoke some words that rendered you great help. This can be included in your correspondence. You can also include some word that you felt was weighty. You can either print or copy these excerpts and mail them to him month by month. In this way you can hold on to these brothers one by one.

If we labor on these two aspects, there will be no problems with brothers who move away. Furthermore, there are places in China where there are no meetings. Sending excerpts by correspondence can be very helpful to those who move to these places. Furthermore, there are brothers who go overseas from Shanghai. They frequently ask us where they can attend meetings. We do not dare tell them where to meet. Their moving away like this can cause them to feel lonely and can be quite dangerous. If they are not guarded by God, there is no way for them to grow. If there is no supply, how can we cause them to grow? Therefore, if these messages can go out continually, we can at least cause the brothers who have moved away to be quite stable. Although their condition may not be excellent, at least they can be fairly stable.

Corresponding with the Receiving Church

My thought is that in the future, regarding the brothers who move away, letters of recommendation can never be the final thing. As the church, after one or two months, we should write a letter to the church where the brother is. We should pay attention to this one thing: Ask them, "Last month a brother was sent to your locality. How is that brother doing now?" We need to ask them to reply. We may say to them in the letter, "We have sent a brother to your locality. How are you helping him? How is the spiritual condition of this brother since he has come into your midst? How are you taking care of him?" If you ask these questions, a lazy church will not be able to answer. Many times people can be lazy. A church can also be lazy. We are afraid of people that are lazy. When we work in this way, many local churches will not be able to be lazy. They must respond. Either they will say, "We are leading him in this way," or they will say, "We are not leading him." If they have never helped him, you can write letters exhorting them that in the future they need to help the brothers who move from other places and that they should pay attention to this matter.

Regarding Brothers from Other Places

Now we come to the care for brothers who come from other places. I hope that many brothers and sisters in our meetings will rise up to serve these saints. This is also one of the duties of a priest. We need to preach the gospel, we need to care for the gospel, we need to care for the new believers, we need to care for problems, we need to care for those who are absent from the meetings, and we need to care for those who come from other places.

Giving This Responsibility to Those Who Care for the Brothers Who Have Moved Away

Those brothers who are responsible for the care of the brothers and sisters who have moved away can at the same time care for the brothers who move from other places. Because these brothers receive the letters from the ones who have moved away, they can realize the difficulties of the brothers who have moved from other places. For instance, thirty brothers move away from Foochow. A group of brothers write to them and they write back. These brothers are able to realize the difficulties in the other places. They especially understand the hardships, the temptations, and the dangers for the brothers who move away. They see this more than anyone and they also know it more clearly. Therefore, it is most convenient to ask these brothers to guide and take care of those who have come into our midst from other places.

The Time Not Needing to Be Long

The length of time for this care may not need to be long. After two or three months, these brothers who have come from other places can be considered as local brothers who can be asked to take care of things on their own. The brothers and sisters who have been responsible for their care can go on to take care of other new ones who have come. If this is not done, they will not be able to take care of everyone. It should always be that each group should make room for the next group. In this way, you can labor on many others.

For example, if two brothers from Tsinan come to Tsingtao, the brothers who take care of this matter need to personally be in fellowship with them for two months. Perhaps they will eventually stop, but within this period of time the brothers must be in fellowship with them. These are the tasks for those who are responsible for taking care of the brothers from other places. If the two brothers want to settle down, other brothers can begin to have particular fellowship with them after two or three months have passed. In this way, the two who came from Tsinan can be turned over to others. After a while, two more brothers may come from the church in Weihaiwai; the brothers who took care of the two who moved to Tsingtao then need to go and take care of them. It should always be group by group, letting some go on the one hand, and picking others up on the other hand. Any special needs or special difficulties need to be taken care of properly. If these matters can be practiced more, there will not be much problem with the brothers who move from other places.

THE WAY OF SERVICE

Not Preferring a Message on the Lord's Day

Brothers, I do not know if you have ever thought about

this. I desire very much to have a heart-to-heart talk with you. Have you seen that Protestantism today emphasizes the messages on Sunday? I feel that this is the problem today. I hope that you can have a thorough consideration these days. Do you want merely to maintain a Lord's Day morning message meeting on the surface? Next year when I go to Tsingtao, Canton, or Peking, I would rather see no messages given on Sunday morning, but rather see each and every brother in Peking serving and each and every brother busy. During the preaching of the gospel, everyone would be there preaching; during the time for taking care of people, everyone would be there taking care of people; during the time of harvest, everyone would be there harvesting; after the harvest, everyone would be there caring for others; when there are matters needing responsibility, there would be brothers there bearing the responsibility. I would say that this is the church. If in a locality there is a very strong Lord's Day morning message meeting, but it is without the service of each and every brother, that is not the church; that is Protestantism. If among us there are four, five, or ten brothers doing well while the rest are immobile, what we have is the priestly system of Catholicism and the pastoral system of Protestantism. That is not the church.

No Inactive Members

The church in the Bible is a church that preaches the gospel, a church that visits people, and a church that cares for others. It is the Body of Christ in a locality. In the Body there are no inactive members. If one day there could be a group of brothers or even a whole church in which everyone serves, everyone carries out spiritual matters properly, everyone bears responsibility, and everyone is busy, then that would be the true Body of Christ.

The Service of the Church Being Our Way Today

Our way today is different than before. We should not consider ourselves to be proper simply because we have done much work and have had many experiences in the past. Today we have turned around completely. We do not recognize

Catholicism! We do not recognize Protestantism! The way of Catholicism and Protestantism is absolutely different from our way. Our way is the service of the church.

I hope you brothers will pay special attention to this matter because when you go to work in different places, it is very easy to forget the vision. It is very easy when the work is heavy to lose the vision. I hope that whenever you work, you will always put the vision before you. It is only when you have the vision that you can work. If you do not see the vision, you will not be able to work. What you have may merely be what you saw two months earlier. Although you feel that the burden is still upon you, it is of no use. The brothers and sisters have not yet risen up, and they are still not working. Therefore, we should not worry about how great the outward difficulties are or how much people talk. The question is whether or not we have genuinely seen our way of service. Because we have seen clearly, we are putting all of our strength into this so that we may cause everyone to work in this way also. If there are many people, thank God; if there are few, it does not matter. The church must take this way.

If there is a local church with two thousand brothers and sisters and only five hundred are serving while fifteen hundred are not serving, it should be strange. If there are five hundred brothers and sisters, then there should be five hundred who serve; otherwise, the brothers will not be able to bear the load.

CHAPTER THREE

THE LEVITICAL SERVICE

We do not need to say much concerning the service of the Levites, because it is a very simple matter. The Levitical work is different from the priestly work. The priests are for serving God and for attending to the things in the tabernacle. The Levites are for serving the priests, helping the priests. In other words, the priestly service represented in the Old Testament is a spiritual service. But the Levitical service refers to the service of practical affairs. The Levites washed the bullocks, poured out the blood, carried away the dung, helped in flaying the offerings, and also carried the things of the tabernacle. Whenever God's pillar of cloud rose up, the tabernacle was taken down, and the Levites came to carry the things of the tabernacle. All these things are the Levitical service.

BEING OF THE WORLD
BUT NOT IN THE WORLD

Although what the Levites do is not spiritual, what they do is related to God and to spirituality; it is of the world but not in the world. The things that they do are in the church. Therefore, in the Bible the service of the deacons is Levitical in nature.

There are deacons in the local churches. The work of the deacons in the local churches is Levitical in nature. They take care of the practical affairs, and these affairs are related to the church.

ALL SHOULD LEARN

With regard to the practical affairs of the church, the brothers and sisters must be very concerned and very clear.

Regardless of what kind of affair it is, all must put their hand to it. For example, the cleaning of the meeting place and the care and arrangement of the blankets and sheets that belong to the church are all in the nature of the service of the Levites. The care of those who are needy among us and the receiving and sending off of visiting brothers and sisters are also work in the nature of the Levitical service. There is a great amount of work in the nature of the Levitical service. There is much work in the church service office, which is also Levitical.

When a person serves God, there is the priestly work on the one hand, and there is the Levitical work on the other hand. Both should be accomplished. On the one hand, you participate in the spiritual service, and on the other hand, you should also take care of the practical affairs. Remember that Stephen and some others took care of serving food. That was the service of the deacons, the work of the Levites. When the disciples distributed the loaves and collected twelve baskets of fragments and on another occasion collected seven baskets of fragments, they were doing the work of the deacons. In particular, Judas's responsibility for the purse was the business of the deacons. The Lord Jesus at the well at Sychar sent His disciples away to buy food. Their buying of food also was the work of the deacons. These things occupy a great part of Christian work. This category of things is what everyone in the church must properly learn before God.

HELPING IN HOUSEHOLD CHORES

Brothers and sisters, at this point I think I can make a suggestion. Please pay close attention to this. There are many brothers and sisters who have some spare time. There are also many sisters at home who have no time whatever. They have to cook, and they have to take care of their children. Why would the brothers in the service of the Levites not take responsibility in this matter by actually arranging for someone to go to their home to help them? The responsible ones can tell them that there are two sisters among us who can help them do the laundry two hours every week. This is also the work of the Levites. At the time of the apostles, the widows of the Hellenists were not adequately being cared for, and there were murmurings. Such was the church. Although this was not something spiritual, but rather a practical affair, it still needed to be done.

TWELVE ITEMS OF PRACTICAL AFFAIRS

There are many things that we can consider before the Lord: (1) the cleaning work; (2) the arranging of the hall and the work of ushering; (3) the need for a group of brothers and sisters to take care of the breaking of bread and the baptisms. Some need to be responsible for the bread and the cup for the bread-breaking meeting. We also need some who are trained to take care of the matters related to baptisms, such as helping those who are being baptized go down and come up out of the water, change their clothes, etc. (4) Giving to the poor among the unbelievers. When unbelievers are involved in disasters of floods or fire, the church should take care of them. (5) Caring for those who are poor among us; (6) the receiving and sending of brothers; (7) the bookkeeping; (8) the kitchen service; (9) the service office; (10) the transportation service. In places where cars or vans are available, some need to oversee their use. (11) The clerical work, which includes handling the incoming and outgoing mail; and (12) helping the poor brothers and sisters do their household chores, including laundry, sewing, mending, etc.

I also expect that every brother and sister will bear the burden in practical affairs. Never let a situation exist where some have things to do and others are doing nothing. The service of the church is always for everyone. If there are some brothers and sisters in our midst who have time, it would be good for them to help other brothers and sisters in their housework. Every week they could go to another brother's or sister's house to help for an hour or two, doing some miscellaneous things for them. Especially, it would be good for those sisters who are housewives with wealth and good standing to go to some brother's or sister's house to do some washing and mending. They should not just have people working for them, while they themselves do nothing.

It befits them as Christians to go to the homes of poor brothers and sisters and do things with their own hands.

THE PRINCIPLE OF EVERYONE SERVING

I have said enough concerning the practical affairs. You have to be clear before God about this principle that all the brothers and sisters must have spiritual service as well as practical service. It does not matter how much everyone can do. I expect that everyone will work and do his best. If this matter can be properly arranged, the church will be able to progress step by step. Brothers, I say again that you must realize that the responsibility upon you is very great and that the things in your hands will keep you very busy. You have to work to such an extent that you bring all the brothers to the same condition that you are in. When all the brothers come and serve together, the church in that locality will have a foundation. When others see this, they will know the church is in our midst. Everyone works, everyone shares in the practical affairs, and everyone participates in the spiritual things.

CAUSING ALL THE ONE-TALENTED ONES
TO DO BUSINESS

I would like to speak to the responsible brothers. You have a natural habit of using only the two-talented ones. The history of the church has always been like this. The five-talented ones can advance by themselves; there is no need to take care of them. But as for the one-talented ones, it is really hard to help them. A word or two to them and they bury their talent again. The two-talented ones are the most available ones. They have some ability, they can do things well, and they do not bury their talents. But if you can use only the two-talented ones and cannot use the one-talented ones in every place, you have failed completely. I have said this in Foochow, I have said this in Shanghai, and I will say it again today. What is the church? The church is all the one-talented ones coming forth to partake of the church service on the practical side and on the spiritual side. You cannot shake your head and say, "This one is useless, and that one is useless." If you say that this one is useless and that one is useless, the church is finished and you fail completely. If you think someone is useless, he will really be useless. You can tell him that according to himself he is indeed useless, but the Lord has given him one talent, and He wants all the one-talented ones to go out and do business. The Lord can use them. If you cannot use the one-talented ones, it proves that before the Lord you cannot be a leader. You have to use all those brothers and sisters who are "useless." This is the job of the brothers who are workers. They must not only use the useful brothers and sisters but also make the useless brothers and sisters useful.

The basic principle is that the Lord has never given less than one talent to anyone. In the Lord's house there is not one servant without a gift; everyone has at least one talent and cannot have less than one talent. No one can excuse himself by saying that the Lord has not given him a talent. I would like you to realize that all of God's children are servants before Him. If they are children, they are servants. In other words, if they are members, they have a gift; if they are members, they are ministers. If we think that there is someone whom the Lord cannot use, we do not know the grace of God at all. We must know the grace of God so thoroughly that when God calls someone His servant, we would never stand up to say that he is not. Today if you did the choosing, perhaps you would pick only three or four persons from the whole church. But God says that all are servants. Since God says this, we must let them serve.

Brothers and sisters, from now on whether or not we have a way in our work and whether or not the way will succeed depend upon what we can say about our work before the Lord. Are there only some who are working? Are only some specially gifted ones doing the work? Or do all the Lord's servants participate in the service, and is the whole church serving? This is the entire problem. If this problem cannot be solved, we have nothing.

THE BODY OF CHRIST BEING LIVING

The Body of Christ is not a doctrine; it is something living.

We all must learn this one thing: Only when every member functions is there the Body of Christ. Only when every member functions is that the church.

Our problem today is that we have inherited the priestly system of Roman Catholicism and the pastoral system of Protestantism. If we are careless at the present time, there will also appear a certain kind of mediatorial system among us. We will be the only ones who take care of the matters in God's service. Merely preaching the Body of Christ is useless; we must let it work and show forth its functions. Since it is the Body of Christ, we need not fear that it will lack the functions. Since it is the Body of Christ, we can place our faith in it. The Lord wants every member in every locality to rise up and serve.

GOD HAVING GONE AHEAD OF US

If I am right, according to my discernment it is possible that the time has come. The letters I have received from different places and the news I have heard from every place indicate that today in every place all the saints are ready to come forth to serve. God has gone ahead of us; we must follow Him.

It is not my desire that even one brother from among us would go out and fail to lead the brothers and sisters to serve but would replace them instead. I hope that when you go to a certain place, you will lead eight or ten to serve at the beginning and then after a certain time they will lead sixty, eighty, or a hundred to serve. Then on your next visit you may see one or two thousand people serving. This is proper. If you must use the five-talented ones to suppress the two-talented ones and the two-talented ones to suppress the one-talented ones, you are not the Lord's servant. If you must use the five-talented ones to replace the two-talented ones and the two-talented ones to replace the one-talented ones, you are not the Lord's servant. You must cause all the five-talented ones to rise up and serve and all the two-talented ones to rise up and serve, and you must also cause all the one-talented ones to rise up and serve. You must also cause those whom you think are not useful to rise up and serve. Thus, the glorious church will appear.

In Foochow I would rather see all the simple villagers serving than three or five outstanding ones preaching. I do not admire the outstanding ones. I like the one-talented ones.

In His graciousness the Lord could give us more Pauls and Peters, but He has not done so. The whole world is full of one-talented brothers and sisters. What shall we do with these people? Where are we going to put them?

PHILADELPHIA MUST APPEAR

In this training here on the mountain, if God really deals with our self and with our work to the extent that we go out to provide a way for all the one-talented ones to serve, for the first time the church will begin to see what brotherly love is and Philadelphia will appear.

Today the church needs not only oversight but also brotherly love. I believe in authority, and I also believe in brotherly love. Without authority the church cannot go on. "And have kept My word"—this is authority. "And have not denied My name"—this is authority. Philadelphia had these two kinds of authority. But Philadelphia herself is brotherly love. All the brothers come forth and serve in love. When such a day comes, we will begin to know what the church is. Otherwise, if the present condition continues, we will still be hanging on to the tail of Roman Catholicism and Protestantism; we will not know what the brothers of Philadelphia are and what the authority of the church is.

TWO WAYS—GIFT AND AUTHORITY

Today I think that two ways are clearly set before us. If the Lord can really break through in our midst, the way we have taken for the past ten, twenty, or thirty years will be completely reversed. Our view cannot be the same as before; it has to be broken and crushed.

Not Leaving Anyone Out

First, you should not use a brother just because he is useful and leave him out if he is not useful. In the church

no member should be left out. This is not the way taken by
the Lord. Today, if the Lord is going to recover His testimony,
He must make all the one-talented ones rise up. All who
belong to the Lord are the members of the Body. Everyone
must rise up and be in his function. If this is the case, you
will see the church. While you are here on the mountain,
consider every place. You almost have to say, "Where is the
church? Where is Christ?" It seems that neither the church
nor the Lord is there. When you go out, never despise the
one-talented ones, never replace them, and never suppress
them. You have to trust them from your heart. You have to
cause them to work. If God has the assurance to call them to
be servants, you too should have the assurance to call them
to be servants.

Authority Dealing with the Flesh

Second, in the church we are not afraid of fleshly
activities. Two lines are to be established in the church—one
is authority and the other is gift. All the one-talented ones
must come forth to serve, work, and bear fruit. You may ask,
"If the one-talented ones come forth with their flesh, what
shall we do?" Let me say that the flesh must be dealt with,
and the way to deal with it is by using the authority which
represents God.

Gift and authority are two entirely distinct things; gift is
gift, and authority is authority. The one-talented ones must
use their gift, and with those who are fleshly, you must use
authority. If a brother brings in the flesh while he is working,
you must tell him, "Brother, that will not do. You cannot bring
that in." Tell him, "This attitude is wrong. We do not allow
you to have this attitude." When you speak with him in this
way, he will probably go home the next day and not do
anything anymore. Then you will have to look him up and
say, "No, you still should do the work." The flesh may come
in again, but you still must let him do the work. You must
say to him again, "You must do this, but we will not allow
you to do that." Always use authority to deal with him.

This is the greatest test. Once the Lord uses the
one-talented ones, their flesh will immediately be brought in.

The flesh and the one talent are joined together. We must refuse the flesh, but we have to use that one talent. Today's situation is that we bury the flesh, they bury the one talent, and the church has nothing. This cannot be! We have to use authority to deal with the flesh, but we also have to ask them to bring forth their talent. Perhaps they will say, "If I work, it will not do, and if I do not work, it will not do either. So what shall I do?" You must say to them, "Indeed, if you work, it is wrong because you bring in the flesh; but if you do not work, it is also wrong because you bury the talent. The one talent must come in, but not the flesh."

In the church if the authority can be maintained and the functions of all the members brought in, you will see a glorious church on the earth, and the way of recovery will be easy. I do not know how many more days the Lord has set before us. I believe our way will be clearer and clearer. We need to use all our thought and all our strength so that all the brothers and sisters may rise up and serve. When that time comes, the church will be manifested and the Lord will return. May the Lord be merciful and gracious to us so that we may do the best.

CHAPTER FOUR

THE MINISTERS OF THE WORD IN THE CHURCH

Today we want to spend some time to see the situation concerning the ministers of the word in the local churches.

NO NEED TO MAINTAIN THE LORD'S DAY MESSAGE MEETING

According to our past custom, the churches in every locality have always maintained the Lord's Day message meeting. In the co-workers' meeting in Hankow, we saw quite clearly that there was no need for a local church to maintain the Lord's Day message meeting, because this kind of meeting is not a church meeting. The messages recorded in *The Normal Christian Church Life* speak concerning this in a very detailed way. The prayer meeting is a meeting of the church. The supplying by the ministers of the word in 1 Corinthians 14 is a meeting of the church. The table meeting is a meeting of the church. The Lord's Day morning preaching meeting, however, is something of Catholicism and Protestantism; it is not a meeting of the church. Actually, it is a meeting of the work rather than a meeting of the church.

The Reason We Could Not Abolish It

Following What the Nations Do

Although there is no need to maintain the preaching on the Lord's Day in a local church, what has been our experience in the ten years since the meetings in Hankow? We are still maintaining the Lord's Day message meeting, following what the nations around us do. It seems that many localities cannot endure the absence of preaching on the Lord's Day. Because the nations around us have preaching on the Lord's Day, we find it hard to relinquish it. We have followed the nations. In the ten years from 1938 to 1948, we have seen that the preaching on the Lord's Day is not a meeting of the local church; what we saw in Hankow was right. However, we have been unable to leave it even until today. What is the difficulty?

Having Nothing to Replace It

I think a big reason for this is that there would be nothing with which to replace it if we abolished the Lord's Day preaching. The nations practice this, so if the brothers in our midst do not, it would be very difficult to maintain the meetings in their localities. Since the people in the denominations listen to a message, we seem to feel that it would be very hard if there were no messages to listen to when they come into our midst on the Lord's Day.

The Result of Not Abolishing It

Still Needing to Build Up the Pastoral System

Therefore, within these few years not one locality has successfully carried out what we saw in Hankow. We still have the problem that we had before the meetings in Hankow. Before the meetings in Hankow, we saw that it is wrong for a brother who is a worker to always remain in the same place. Brothers who are workers should be scattered to many localities. But today it seems that a worker still needs to live in a particular place in order to maintain the Lord's Day message meeting. As long as we need to maintain the Lord's Day message meeting, we build up the pastoral system. If we need to maintain the Lord's Day message meeting, then there is the need for a worker to live in a place to do that work, since local brothers have no way of maintaining the Lord's Day message meeting. I hope that when you brothers have time, you will again read the messages given in *The Normal Christian Church Life*. The meetings for edification, the table meetings, the prayer meetings, and the gospel preaching meetings are all meetings of the church, but maintaining the Lord's Day message meeting is the behavior of the nations and not something of the church. We admit our failure of the past ten years; we cannot be proud.

The Problem with Not Abolishing It

The Outward Problem—
Desiring to Listen to Messages

Why have we not practiced what we saw in the past ten years? There are reasons for this, one inward and the other outward. The outward reason is that all the nations have a Lord's Day message meeting, and if we do not have one among us, we fear that without a message to listen to many brothers and sisters will go to other places to listen to messages. However, if this is the case, we should realize how few are the priests among us. Many among us still want to be those who are served, and we are not able to be those who serve. To be a priest is not a matter of being served, but a matter of serving. To be one who listens to messages is to be served, not to serve. This is the outward problem.

The Inward Problem—Having a Habit

The inward problem is that if there is not a Lord's Day message meeting, many brothers and sisters, after being Christians for ten or twenty years, will feel that this is absolutely different from their former habit as Christians. They will feel that being a Christian today is different from what it was in the past. This is also a problem.

The Need to See Accurately

Today I want to discuss with the brothers and sisters what we should do concerning this matter. The words that I speak here are only suggestions, not my preaching, because we must see accurately before we can practice.

A Local Church Not Maintaining
the Lord's Day Message Meeting

To this day I have not been able to find the Lord's Day message meeting once in the Bible. Especially in a local church, you can see that there is no way to maintain a Lord's

Day message meeting. If a local church wants to strengthen the Lord's Day message meeting, then it must have a worker. Whether you call him a worker or a pastor, it is the same. There is still someone to maintain the Lord's Day message meeting.

Always Abolishing the Class
of Those Who Want to Be Served

What has our situation become? Among us we do not believe in the priestly system. We are all priests. We do not believe in the priestly system disguised as the clergy system, we do not believe in the priestly system disguised as the pastoral system, and neither do we believe in the priestly system disguised as a system of workers. Hence, if we do not resolve this matter, when we go out, we cannot expect to be able to work in a proper way. We must learn to raise up all the brothers and sisters to be priests. When all come to serve, those among us who are being served will decrease. We must abolish the class of those who are being served. If there are still those who are being served and who expect others to be the priests while they remain simply as God's people, there will never be a way to eliminate the Lord's Day message meeting. There will never be a way to have the representation of the Body in that locality, because there will always be those who are passive, who listen to others speak, and who do not speak themselves. If the church wants to be successful as the church and successful as the Body of Christ in a locality, then the entire Body must serve. The service of the entire Body is that all the people, whether five-talented, two-talented, or one-talented, rise up to serve God. Please remember, this is the requirement for a group to become the Body of Christ.

The Way of the Church

Working Replacing Listening to Messages

I believe that the way of the church is as follows: Save and gain a person from outside, and after he is saved, immediately put him into the work so as not to produce the habit of listening to messages on the Lord's Day. We need to change to the habit of working on the Lord's Day. I believe that our failure over these ten years will be completely changed from today. In these ten years we have taught that it is right for the saints to have the habit of listening to messages on the Lord's Day; we have not replaced it with something. We did not substitute preaching with working on the Lord's Day. Today we have found that working on the Lord's Day is what should be done and what is proper. Because our practice has not been proper, that which is wrong has come in.

The Entire Body Being Mobilized to Preach the Gospel

If the churches in every locality cause all the one-talented members to rise up and to stand and work, it is very possible that we can return to the situation of the early church. The Lord's Day mornings should be used to preach the gospel. The Lord's Day is the time for everyone to be mobilized to save people. You have to gather the new believers and let them know that every Lord's Day is the day on which all of us are busy. We must preach the gospel every Lord's Day.

No doubt the church on the earth needs to be fed. I believe in feeding, and I also believe that in China there is no one who believes in feeding as I do. However, I admit that the mission of the church on the earth is not feeding but the preaching of the gospel. Therefore, we need to use every Lord's Day for the preaching of the gospel, whether in the morning or in the afternoon, but especially in the morning because this is the time when everyone everywhere "goes to worship." We will have a message meeting every Lord's Day morning, but it will be for the gospel.

All of the brothers must go out to lead people to the meeting. We can also have advertisements, but we do not stress this. We can use other methods, but we should stress the need for one to invite two and another to invite four. By working in this way, we will immediately see that all will be busy, because all the brothers and sisters will be preaching the gospel and saving people. We should not only do this on the Lord's Day, but we must go to seek out people and talk with them at other times, and we must also bring them to hear the gospel and seek out new ones to come and listen. If we bring many people, we will have to find others to help care for them. This kind of work in the care of the gospel is the primary work of the brothers and sisters.

If we lead people to believe and be saved every Lord's Day, it will not be long before the brothers' habit of listening to messages will be gone. Then the true nature of the church will be manifested. Who are the ones called church members? They are those who listen to messages on the Lord's Day. But after a period of time, their nature will be changed. Eventually, everyone who goes out to preach the gospel and save people will be called a church member. He who actively goes out to save people will be called a church member, a Christian. There will no longer be a passive habit of listening to messages.

The Whole Church Being Priests

You must see what the church is. I believe the light is very clear now: The church is everyone being a priest. This type of universal priesthood has been preached for more than a hundred years. From 1828 until today, a period of one hundred twenty years, the eyes of God's servants have been opened to see that the priesthood is universal. However, even today the priesthood is still not widespread. The church is the Body of Christ. The recovery of this testimony has been going on for more than one hundred years. Of course, within the last ten or more years some have especially seen its spiritual weight. However, in the church it is very possible that the Body of Christ is still merely a doctrine. In actuality we are far from bringing it into the church life.

Every Member Functioning

Therefore, you need to ask God to open your eyes to cause you to know what the Body is. The Body is every member functioning. In the body there is not one member that does not function; likewise, there is not one person who belongs to the Lord who is not a priest serving the Lord. All the members function. All the priests serve.

Being Able to Find the Church Everywhere

After you go out, you should completely change the brothers' and sisters' way of thinking. Formerly, they thought that there were many workers in the church. Today we need to turn this around and say that everyone in the church is a worker. I have said before and I repeat it today, you have to speak this kind of word until one day everyone understands it inwardly. If the church does not endeavor until everyone in the church is working and everyone in the church is serving, then there is no church. If the whole church rises up to work and serve, you will immediately see the Body of Christ. Everywhere there will be three or five or seven or eight people serving God; you will be able to find the church everywhere.

However, once you have gone down from the mountain, I do not expect you to eliminate the preaching on the Lord's Day and change immediately. There can be no such thing! It is a matter of working until we reach that point.

In the Morning Serving Man; in the Evening Serving God

I do not know if you have seen this vision. Let me tell you how wonderful it would be if one day in the mind of God's children there was no thought of attending worship services. We could eliminate this manner of listening to messages and, instead, have the entire church serve according to God's word in the Bible. The Lord's Day mornings would be for all the priests to serve man, and the Lord's Day evenings would be for all the priests to serve God. On the Lord's Day mornings whether or not you go to a meeting would not matter. It would also be acceptable to change the day of the gospel meeting to another day. The Lord's Day mornings should always be for the priests to go and serve man; everyone must serve man. On the Lord's Day evening everyone should serve God, offering up sacrifices. When you see such a people, then the church will be as it should be. When you can see that all the believers, once they are saved,

are for the Lord, have the thought of saving others, and are
working and caring for people, then you can really see the
church.

Working after Being Saved

Once a person is saved, he should always consider whom
he should bring to salvation. Once a person is saved, he should
be one who works; once a person is saved, he should be one
who testifies. I do not know whether or not you have seen
this. We must lead people to the point that the church is as
it should be before God. I want to speak a very frank word.
Today in the church the persons are right, but the situation
is indeed wrong. The persons belong to God, the persons are
right, but the situation is completely wrong. The situation is
passive.

Therefore, when you go down from this mountain, you
need to change not only the way of the work, so that now
you have a definite center, but also the nature of the work.
What is the nature of the work? It is to lead people to begin
to work from the moment they are saved. The workers must
lead the brothers to work and must not replace them by doing
the work.

From now on there should not be much difference between
the workers and the brothers, except that your spiritual
condition before the Lord is strong, while theirs perhaps is
weaker. In the matter of the work there is no difference,
because they also are co-workers. It is only when you reach
this point that you can understand the New Testament.
The entire New Testament regards all of God's children as
co-workers, because they all are working. The only difference
is that you have been sent to work, you have presented all of
your time and energy, and you have been sent to different
places to work. I especially want you to see this matter.

Being Able to Overthrow Our Tradition

If within you are capable and strong enough, you will
always push and always work, and you will be able to tear
down our entire tradition.

The weight of tradition is very heavy. This tradition is

oppressing. If you want to overthrow it, you must use considerable strength. This is not something quick. It will take a year or two before you can produce a new situation.

THE SUPPLY OF THE WORD

Let us first speak concerning the supply of the word. Then we will come back and talk about the way of the church.

The Supply of the Word
for Edifying New Believers

Regarding the ministry of the word, for now we will use the following arrangement: We will have fifty-two topics for the regular year. In addition, we will have one or two topics on the side for use in the leap years. Please remember, when we are strong in the matter of preaching the gospel, many will be saved. Once many have been saved, there will be more trouble for the church because all kinds of people will come in. All kinds of fish will be pulled into the boat; therefore, we will need to take good care of them, providing the new believers with edification once a week.

We do not plan to change the topics for the meeting for edifying new believers. Every local church in every locality will speak the same topic on every Thursday or Friday. Tsingtao will do this; Shanghai will do this; Foochow will also do this. Every locality will be working in the same steps. From now on we do not plan to modify the topics used in the meeting for edifying new believers. It will not be one way this year and another way next year. We desire that every group of new believers that comes in would receive the same edification by being brought together in each locality every Thursday or Friday. We need to spend an entire year to touch all the main matters in the Word of God and the way to be a Christian. In this way there will be no lack with respect to the supply of the word for the new believers. Do not be afraid that something might be lacking if there is no Lord's Day message meeting. At least with respect to the new believers, there will be no lack; the supply will still be there.

I hope that the brothers who go out to work will not change these topics, but simply work accordingly. If you want to change, let us wait until our next gathering to discuss how to make adjustments. Today I believe the topics which we have selected are already prevailing enough and sufficient to supply them.

Once we have the work related to the gospel, plus the fifty-two topics for the edification of the new believers, I believe it will be very easy to meet the need of a local church regarding the matters of the faith and our conduct. In this way the brothers will not need to search everywhere for food.

The Word and the Anointing Being Repeated

If you are living, then these things will be living. If you are dead before God, these things will become like publicly recited prayers; they will become dead things. If all of you are living, then even that which is dead will become living. If all of you are dead before God, even the living things will become dead, even a book as living as the Gospel of John. In the same way, if you are living, I believe that by speaking the things we have arranged year after year, both the words and the anointing can be repeated. The words can be repeated, and the life can also be repeated. In this way you can edify the new believers.

The Supply for the Gospel and the Supply for Edification

Now you have seen that there are two meetings. The first is the Lord's Day morning gospel meeting, stressing gospel preaching for saving people. Once some have been saved and brought in, you must pay attention before God to give the new believers a clear leading in the word. The Lord's Day morning supply of the word is related to the gospel. The supply of the word on Thursday or Friday night is related to edification.

The Supply of the Word in 1 Corinthians 14

Some may ask how we should supply the older brothers, and many other brothers and sisters among us, with the word. This is the purpose of the Saturday night meeting, the meeting for the exercise of the spiritual gifts. This meeting is conducted according to 1 Corinthians 14. In this meeting each one has a word, has a revelation, has a hymn, has a prayer.

If today some feel that the meeting for edifying new believers is not sufficient, please remember that every Saturday night you can let several able ministering brothers take care of a stronger and fresher meeting. Every Lord's Day morning we have to preach the gospel and every Thursday we must have the meeting for edifying new believers. Perhaps every Saturday night we will have an additional meeting according to 1 Corinthians 14, in which we can supply God's children with God's word. Either one, two, or three can speak. The Saturday night meetings have to be very living, not like today's Lord's Day message meeting, which is maintained in a dead way. Today maintaining the Lord's Day message meeting is quite hard even for a worker because if he has a word, he must speak, and if he does not have a word, he still must speak. It is also very hard for a local brother to maintain because, similarly, if he has a word, he must speak, and if he does not have a word, he also must speak.

But if we do not maintain the Lord's Day message meeting today, the brothers and sisters will be scattered. It is as if we use the Lord's Day morning meeting to bind the brothers and sisters together. I hope that what binds them together from now on will not be the Lord's Day message meeting, but the gospel preaching work. What will bind them together is everyone testifying, everyone preaching the gospel, and everyone saving people. If we get them accustomed to working, and they move to another locality, they will feel that they cannot do without the opportunity to work. We must give every brother the opportunity to work, lead everyone to have a habit to work, and lead everyone to have a habit to preach the gospel. Then we will have a church in a locality that is very stable.

For example, in a locality on every Lord's Day morning, there will be a gospel meeting with different brothers taking turns to be responsible for one or two months with some arrangement before God. That will be a corporate gospel preaching, corporately leading people to be saved. When someone is saved and receives the Lord, you then may bring him to the Thursday night meeting. After being there for a year he will have received his basic edification. Those who are burdened for the word and those who have a burden before God and are not passive will stand up on Saturday nights to speak.

Everyone Being Responsible

Today there are many localities where the Saturday night meetings cannot be strong because all the brothers are passive, even though many are gifted with a ministry. If there is no pressure on them, as with the Lord's Day meetings which force them to go before God, then every Saturday night meeting will be a time to relax. If all the brothers relax, bearing no responsibility, how can the meeting be strong? If no one bears the burden, how can the meeting be strong? We should not allow anyone to be passive! Who then would take the initiative? The meeting according to 1 Corinthians 14 is not a meeting where everyone shirks responsibility; the meeting in 1 Corinthians 14 is a meeting in which everyone bears responsibility. For one person to bear the responsibility is wrong; for no one to bear the responsibility is also wrong.

Having Half an Hour of Prayer
and Preparation Beforehand

Now I want to talk about how the responsible brothers in each locality should carry out the Saturday night meetings. The Saturday night meetings are the same as the other meetings in that the responsible brothers should pray together. Before every meeting the responsible brothers should arrive at least half an hour early to have some prayer. It should be the same with the gospel meetings, the meetings for edifying new believers, the prayer meetings, and the bread-breaking meetings. The responsible brothers should always be there half an hour or fifteen minutes early to have some prayer and preparation. Especially for the Saturday night meetings, you may need a little more time. You should usually arrive fifteen minutes early, but for this meeting you need to arrive half an hour early. You have to ask the responsible brothers to come for half an hour of prayer first, and then you need to help them to the extent that even if others have not prepared, they would be prepared. The responsible brothers can enter into the meeting only when they have the assurance before God. There should be no responsible brother who can simply remove his hat and rush into the meeting. Every responsible brother must first have some preparation before he can go in.

There are many localities with many unspiritual persons who want to occupy the podium. You need to pray much for them so that they would not come in and control the podium. Those that enter in should be the ones who have a genuine burden before God, those who are fearful of having a poor meeting. Hence, you need to pray beforehand and then take good care of the meeting so that it may be uplifted.

Those Who Are Apt to Teach
Needing to Bear More Responsibility

The responsible brothers should especially pray regarding the Saturday night meeting. You need to ask whether there are brothers among you who are particularly burdened. This does not mean that the ministering of the word is limited to responsible brothers. However, we must admit that the responsible brothers should bear more of the responsibility in ministering the word. The elders are for serving the church, and even though they are not for the ministry of the word, they should be apt to teach. Therefore, when all those who are apt to teach are gathered together, they should ask whether anyone has a special burden before God that night, whether there is a particular burden (even though everyone should be burdened), and whether there is anyone with a special word to say. Every time you come to the Saturday night meeting, there should be at least a few responsible brothers who are not passive. When the responsible brothers are passive, everyone becomes passive.

I am amazed that often three to five brothers are ministers of the word before God, but they think that they can open up the Saturday night meetings for other brothers to speak. When the meeting does not turn out well, they shake their heads and say that the meeting was not good. If the mouth does not speak and the nose goes to speak, it is no wonder that the voice is not clear. This is often the problem. When it comes to the fellowship meeting or a meeting according to 1 Corinthians 14, many brothers who can bear responsibility do not do anything, yet they criticize. This is a strange thing.

The Supply of the Apostles' Word

The supply of the apostles' word is the supply of the ministers of the word. The gospel preaching and the edifying of new believers in the regular meetings should be sufficient for the brothers to have the habit of serving in the gospel and edifying the new believers. If we desire a stronger supply of the word, then we need meetings such as those in 1 Corinthians 14. This is the case in a local church. Then what is the responsibility of an apostle? During a certain time, when a brother passes by a certain locality, he should stay for a few days as Paul did when he passed through Troas and stayed for seven days. You may stay there for a few days, a week, or a month and hold a conference. Perhaps a local church or several local churches in the area may join together two or three times to get some special help.

The Lord's Day Message Meeting Being a Waste

I have considered before God many times for many years, and I deeply believe that the help rendered to people by the Lord's Day morning preaching cannot match what God desires to do. Frankly speaking, if we are not careful, the Lord's Day preaching will become a waste and a loss. It is best to turn that message into gospel work. The Lord's Day is the time for everyone to be mobilized to go out to save people. Thursday is the time for all the new believers to be edified, and perhaps Saturday is the time for the brothers and sisters to be gathered together to be mutually edified. On special occasions in a locality, an apostle may have a three to five-day conference. After finishing, he may go to another place to have a three to five-day conference. In this way you will see that the church will be very balanced in the matter of the supply of the word, and her way will be straight.

Today we are not talking about the locality which is the center of the work, but the localities outside the center of the work. They cannot bear the burden of a Lord's Day message meeting. Once this burden is present, you almost have to place a worker there. Once you do this, you have quite a problem. This is the time every brother should rise up to serve God. We cannot have a system of workers.

The pressure of tradition is very strong. When we first begin to push against it, it is very heavy. The pressure on my spirit is heavy. We need to push against it day after day. After two or three years the situation will change. Then all the brothers and sisters will desire to have the gospel preaching work on the Lord's Day. If you say, "Let us preach a message to you," no one will want to listen to your message. They will see immediately that this is not the church. If, after two years, you send these brothers and sisters to another place or another church and ask them to listen to messages, they will not be able to sit still. They will sense that they should not be there, that their being there makes them just like members of Catholicism, where everything is done by a priest and where they could not have a portion.

Needing to Walk the Way of Recovery

The situation of the church today is altogether not according to the New Testament! Therefore, we need to reverse it. God wants to take the way of recovery; we also need to take the way of recovery. We should always lead the brothers and sisters to the point where they are the ones working and serving. There is service toward the sinners, and there is also service toward the new believers. Among them there is also the mutual edifying as in 1 Corinthians 14, that is, help rendered mutually by the saints from the word before God.

If you live in a locality for a while, you can add your portion of the word to the Saturday meetings. Even if you are not a worker, you can still add your portion of the word to the Saturday meetings.

If there is a need for further spiritual supply, we can immediately release many workers to go out and travel from place to place. Formerly, you fixed them one by one in a single place, but today it should not be so. They must be mobile, going from one place to another. They should go out, being in one place for three to five days and in another place for three to five days.

Not Needing Highly Gifted Persons

If we work in this way, I believe that the situation in every locality will be very balanced, and we do not know how many times the increase in numbers will be multiplied. It is a great thing, a most wonderful thing, for the church to preach the gospel! For the church to preach the gospel in the Lord's Day meeting is the most glorious work! If we can have a breakthrough in the way of the Lord's recovery at this time, if the church can rise up to preach the gospel, there will be the dawning of a new day everywhere. This does not mean that there must be a few highly gifted persons in the church, such as Philip or Charles Stanley, Whitefield, or Wesley. The power of the church's gospel preaching is much greater than their power!

If we want a five-talented member to be manifested, it may take twenty or even fifty years to produce one. How difficult that would be! But if we take the five worst brothers here in Kuling and put them together, there will be five talents. If we put the five least spiritual ones together, there will also be five talents. If we expect to see a five-talented member rise up, we will realize that there are not very many in the church. But if the church preaches the gospel, then the effect will not be that of only five five-talented members, but that of ten, one hundred, one thousand, or ten thousand five-talented members. Moreover, we will continue to see this effect everywhere. Whether or not the gospel can get through is not a matter of preaching by the workers, it is a matter of preaching by the church. The church will overturn the world.

The Work Being Placed upon the Church

Therefore, today before God you must see this vision

accurately. Your view must be accurate, and you must thoroughly see the Lord's spiritual revelation. "O Lord, You place the work on the church." The Head directs the Body, not individual members. It is necessary that the entire Body develop all of its strength. Therefore, I desire that there would be the local representations of the Body in China. Do not think that the Body of Christ is something in the heavens. Looking for a local church in the heavens would be idealistic. You must see that the Body of Christ is manifested on the earth. The Body of Christ is spiritual to the point that it can be manifested on the earth.

The Supply of the Word Being Very Important

Since this is the case, you can see that the supply of the word is very important. We need to preach the gospel, edify the new believers, and have mutual and special edifying. Therefore, many, including the sisters, need to go out, group by group, in twos or threes, so that every locality may be able to stand on its own.

Without this, today's problem will remain. There will still be a need to maintain a Lord's Day message meeting. You have to overturn this habit of listening to messages. You must overturn it completely. The Lord's Day is the time for all of us to go out and save people. If this habit is overturned, it will be impossible to ask the brothers and sisters to just listen to a message on the Lord's Day.

Perhaps there will be times when we pause for a while and have a conference for a whole week. If co-workers come, we will have a feast for one whole week, and then we will go out to work again. In these few years I have especially seen what God has done in the hearts of brothers everywhere. Gradually, the church must preach the gospel and do the work. This way is already quite clear.

New Believers Needing to Migrate

You will probably ask what the new believers should do in the second year after listening for a year to the fifty-two topics, which neither advance nor change. The answer is that you need to send them out in migrations. If not, we will definitely have to build a "Solomon's Temple," because there will not be a place that is large enough to meet in.

Therefore, after a group of believers has been raised up at the end of a year, you have to deal with them concerning their going on. They then will care for new believers. At the same time, you have to cause them to see that living on the earth is for preaching the gospel and for the Lord's interest; they cannot choose their own professions or their own places to live. Thus, we will see that we can send out five hundred or a thousand people after one or two years. If a place does not have the church, there will be a church there after one or two hundred people have been sent out. After a few years we can send many out to places where the gospel has not yet come. We must send them out group by group.

The Migrations Also Being a Way to Preach the Gospel

In Acts there are two different ways of preaching the gospel: one way is that of Antioch, sending apostles out to preach the gospel. The church has paid special attention to this way throughout these years. However, Jerusalem had another way of preaching the gospel which was different from that of Antioch. Jerusalem's way of preaching the gospel was that of sending out a group of people through migration to preach the gospel after they were saved. After reading chapters eight, ten, eleven, and twelve of Acts, you will then realize that whether they went out because of persecution or whether they went out according to arrangement, the migrations for the preaching of the gospel were always right. As soon as one is saved he should go out. It would also be good if among us there were three to five brothers and sisters who wanted to go to preach the gospel to a certain primitive tribe. If, in a certain place such as Jerusalem, many have been saved, you must then send them out. If you do not send them out, persecution may come. When you send people out, you will find that they will go to preach the gospel. Workers, we should never think that people are always gained by the workers. Sometimes, the workers go out and gain people, but sometimes the sent-out saved ones gain people. We must take both of these ways. If we can carry out migrations on a large scale, I believe that it will not be many years before we take China. If, as before, we are saving people one by one, there will be no way to do this even after a thousand years. Today the total number in China who claim to believe, not counting Catholics, is merely a few hundred thousand Protestants, perhaps six hundred thousand. After more than one hundred years of gospel preaching, there are only six hundred thousand! Among these six hundred thousand, we do not know how many are saved. Therefore, if God will work here, I believe there will be a prevailing way for the gospel to go out.

Needing to Change Our Habit

Therefore, you need to see that the supply of the word in a locality is already sufficient. At the same time, the former habit also needs to be changed. This is a basic requirement. As soon as a person is saved, he should not be one who desires to come and listen to messages. Rather, he should be one who realizes the need to work right away, to preach the gospel right away, and to save people right away, carrying out these things without delay before God and hurrying to save people.

The Need for New Apostles to Rise Up

At the same time, if we want to be strong in the matter of preaching the gospel, we need new apostles to rise up. This is the purpose of Kuling. If you find new brothers and sisters who are able to go on, you must send them here when they have learned something of this way after two or three years. We will coordinate with you. We will ask them to live here for one or two years. Then we will send them out and let them begin to work from place to place. I hope we can coordinate and go on in a good way. I believe this matter is a great thing.

Regarding the supply of the word in a local church, I hope that we would not make the Lord's Day message meeting our center. If the Lord's Day message meeting continues to occupy the central position in a local church, there will be no way for the gospel to advance. We must allow two or three brothers to rise up in every local church to preach the gospel on the Lord's Day and continue this work there. The rest of the brothers and sisters will continue to help. I believe that all of the former problems will go away. We might have problems in other areas, but there will be no problems in the area of preaching the gospel. Once we have the preaching of the gospel, all the other problems will also be easy to resolve.

What to Do in the Place
Where the Center of the Work Is

What shall we do with the locality where the center of the work is? I believe that the local church at the center of the work also needs to have these several kinds of meetings. However, if the locality where the center of the work is desires to maintain a Lord's Day meeting, I am not personally against that. I do not know how you brothers feel. This is one issue that I wish to discuss with you. Perhaps we will reverse the situation. Formerly, we preached the gospel once a month; now once a month we preach a message to the brothers, or if there is a strong ministry of the word, perhaps we will select one day out of the week and use it specifically for preaching a message. Perhaps, we will preach the gospel every Lord's Day morning and have the ministry of the word in the afternoon.

My personal feeling is that we do not need to immediately eliminate the message meeting in the locality where the center of the work is. I have spoken about this previously, but it was not clear. What I am saying is that our direction has to be accurate. Then we can work gradually, step by step, until the brothers and sisters see that the Lord's Day is the day for our service, particularly the service of the gospel. The situation from locality to locality is not the same. We should not immediately endeavor to stop having the message meeting; rather, we should observe the situation and make arrangements gradually to lead the brothers into this way. At a certain point we will see that working can replace listening to the messages.

More Emphasis Being Given at the Apostles' Time to Preaching the Gospel than to Listening to Messages

When we read the book of Acts, we must see that at that time there were not as many ministers of the word as we have now. At that time God's children probably paid more attention to preaching the gospel than to listening to messages. However, today it seems that the basic factor of being a Christian is listening to messages rather than preaching the gospel. Therefore, I hope that we can see this way very accurately and thoroughly. We must lead the brothers in every locality into this way. We must carry it out to such an extent that all the brothers and sisters are preaching the gospel before taking care of other matters. If this way can be carried out, the number of those saved in the past will not be comparable to the number that will be saved. At the same time, there will be no need to maintain so many workers in every place, and we will also begin to see churches rising up.

I thank God that Romans 12 says that he who exhorts should attend to exhorting and he who teaches should attend to teaching, but Romans 12 does not say that he who listens to messages should attend to listening to messages. If those who listen to messages attend to listening to messages, then the church will be brought to naught. There is no such thing as attending to listening to messages. To listen to messages is not a function of the Body. We need to ask God to give us grace so that every child of God may rise up to serve and preach the gospel.

When you practice this, I hope that you will hold fast to your direction. It is your own responsibility before God as to how you will turn your way around and how much time it will take. You must take good care of the saints in order to lead them into this way, not quickly dropping one thing and quickly picking up another. There should be no such thing. You must always preach in this way and work in this way. If you come to the point where the brothers and sisters have risen up, then make the change. You must see that the Lord's Day morning is their busiest time. It is not a time for old and young, men and women to come hand in hand to listen to a message. Rather, it is a time for everyone to come to preach the gospel.

The Vision of the Work

The work in every place today has not been carried out well. It is in the initial stages. However, the vision is before you. From now on you need to work in this way every day. Only after we reverse the direction will we be right. If all the brothers and sisters have not yet risen up, you must continue working until they all rise up to work and preach the gospel. It should always be the church that serves and preaches the gospel. This way is right, and this is the New Testament church.

The Need to Rise Up to Build the Temple

Please remember that Catholicism is the church in captivity in Babylon. Many Bible readers admit this. As the children of Israel were taken captive to Babylon, the church was also taken captive to Babylon. Protestantism came back from Babylon, but they did not build the temple. Even though many came back from Babylon, the temple was not there. Today you and I must be those in church history who rise up to build the temple. We are a people like Nehemiah, building the temple and learning to raise up God's church again in this age. Many have come out of Babylon but still have a Babylonian appearance. Even today they still do not look like the church. Catholicism is very structured. Protestantism is less structured, but being less structured is still not the church. In order for there to be a local church, the church must preach the gospel and the church must serve. Within the next few years, I hope to repeat these two phrases ten thousand times: The church needs to preach the gospel and the church needs to serve. Only then is it the church; otherwise, it is an incomprehensible gathering, very much unlike the church.

Brothers, in the beginning it will indeed be hard. But you need to see the vision accurately and clearly. What is the church? Being the church requires that we preach the gospel as the church; being the church requires that we serve as the church. Therefore, responsible brothers and sisters, you need to gather together often to discuss and to pray: "O Lord, how can we cause all of the brothers and sisters to rise up?" Our way is not that we ourselves always put our hands to the work, but that we cause others to work. It is wrong for us to take care of everything while the brothers and sisters do nothing. It should be that we work with the purpose of leading them to work. If we work in order to induce them to come out and work, this is correct. They must be busy. We should place each one of them, making arrangements so that everyone is preaching the gospel and serving. At that time we will realize that this way is correct.

The Church Always Needing to Be in the Freedom of the Holy Spirit

I think that in the local churches the service in the word is already adequate. These few points are sufficient to meet the local need. Concerning the mutual edifying in 1 Corinthians 14, if the local brothers are strong, the Saturday night meetings will be strong. If the local brothers are not strong, the Saturday night meetings will not be strong. I think every child of God must admit that the strongest supply of the word was that which was among the Brethren a century ago. This is something amazing. Why was the supply of the word so strong and so abundant in the last century? It was because they were working according to the principle of 1 Corinthians 14. The Holy Spirit had freedom there. Even though they had much insignificant speaking, they also had much substantial speaking. Without this principle they could not have had what they had at that time. Therefore, during the Saturday night meetings, even though many who should not speak will rise up, there will also be the opportunity for those who should speak to speak. Once the Holy Spirit has the freedom, you can expect the Holy Spirit to speak in the church and operate in the church. The church must always be in the freedom of the Holy Spirit.

2 Kinds of meetings:-
ministry meeting - one man speaking
church meeting - all saints speaking
- training meeting - for work, ministry

CHAPTER FIVE

THE DIFFERENT KINDS OF MEETINGS IN THE CHURCH

THE GOSPEL PREACHING MEETING

In the church there are different kinds of meetings. The gospel preaching meeting is one kind of meeting. The local brothers should find a special time for the gospel preaching meeting, perhaps the Lord's Day morning, to gather together to preach the gospel or to go to various districts to preach the gospel. Always preach the gospel with all your strength.

When you have a gospel preaching meeting, as we have already mentioned, you need to bring people with you. You need to sit with the people you have brought. If you bring two people, you should sit between them and keep them company. You should also talk to them and listen to the message with them. After they finish listening, accompany them home. You should follow up on them until they are baptized.

The preaching of the gospel message should be done in a strong way. At the same time, we need two or three brothers to do their best to send gospel material to the meetings of various localities. We need to compile gospel stories, gospel illustrations, and things which have been used in the past, and send them out so that the various localities will have materials for gospel preaching. By doing so, the meetings in various localities will receive much benefit.

At the same time, the attitude of the brothers while listening to the message in a gospel preaching meeting has to be right. Many times it is our own brothers who ruin the meeting. The brothers need to realize that the gospel is not preached for them to hear. You need to help that meeting and not cause it to become weak, and you need to learn to lead the people who sit next to you to believe in the gospel. Of course you do not need the gospel. But they do. It is much easier on the gospel preacher if the attitude of all the brothers in the gospel preaching meeting is right. Otherwise, the person who preaches the gospel must be concerned about the sinners and also about the reaction of the brothers. You need to realize that he is not here taking a test on gospel preaching, but he is doing his best to get people saved. If everyone would do this, the gospel preaching meeting would have few difficulties.

I hope that the gospel preaching meeting is not too long or too short. To preach for an hour or two is no problem.

Two-thirds of the time of the gospel preaching meeting is always for casting the net, and one-third is for drawing the net. This is a good way to take.

THE MEETING FOR THE EDIFICATION OF THE NEW BELIEVERS

The subject of this meeting is definite; therefore, the preaching also has to be definite.

In every local church you have to find two or three brothers to preach the word in this meeting. There should always be two or three such brothers in a meeting. Sometimes a brother may not feel well or may be absent for other reasons; another brother may then speak in his place.

When the meeting becomes large, divide it into several districts. At this point, there should be a few more brothers responsible for the edification of the new believers.

I hope that the topics used for the edification of the new believers will not be changed, but will be repeated each year. I also hope that the topics and the order of the topics spoken in various places are uniform. Every week there should be speaking on the same topic so that when a person goes to any locality, he can still continue to attend this meeting without interruption. If he goes from Shanghai to Hangchow, he can continue. If he goes from Hangchow to Canton, he can also continue. And if he goes from Canton to Hong Kong, he can still continue. Thus, a new believing brother may be able to continue wherever he goes. In this way he can receive edification in many subjects.

These few years we have realized one thing: The edification that the brothers in our midst have received is not the same; it is really different! Therefore, there is considerable difficulty. This time when I took a trip to the inland area, I had many impressions, even deep impressions. In many places there are those who claim to be brothers among us, who are also quite polite and quite good. I feel that they are brothers. But I found out that they have not even learned the ABC's. Therefore, many problems have occurred in those places, and difficult situations arose. For this reason, I hope that starting from today, the meeting for the edification of the new believers will be carried out properly. This meeting will enable all the new believing brothers to acquire the basic lessons.

Being Careful to Make Up Lessons

In the meeting for the edification of the new believers, there is one point that we need to pay attention to. Those who are responsible for visiting the new believers must learn these topics well. Otherwise, when they go out, they will not be able to help the new believers make up the lessons. I hope the brothers could realize this problem. Perhaps the new believers' message is an hour and a half long. However, when they make up lessons for the new believers, they finish it in two minutes. It is not that they speak just the outline; they speak an outline of the outline. I remember that some brothers, when they made up lessons for others, spoke just one sentence: "The message for the new believers today says that we need to read the Bible every day." They did not say anything wrong; what they said was correct. But when you go to a person's home to make up lessons, if you only speak a sentence such as, "You need to read the Bible every day," I think this word is equivalent to not speaking anything, unless the Holy Spirit works in a special way. You should not speak just one sentence; you must be trained to speak carefully paragraph by paragraph so that those who listen may feel as if they have gone to a meeting. Otherwise, the loss is quite great.

Please remember that after the gospel has been preached, the future condition of our meetings depends on whether or not the new believers' edification meeting is strong. There are those in our midst who have just heard the gospel. If the meeting for the edification of the new believers is not strong, then we have no way to meet their need. We must learn to lead them onward. How strong the new believers' meeting is determines how strong the next generation will be. If you cannot help the new believers' meeting to be strong, the next generation cannot be strong. Yes, the people have all believed in the gospel and are all saved, but there is no church. That is something similar to what a revival meeting does. There is preaching and there is a result, but no church.

The Teaching and the Fellowship of the Apostles

I want you to especially remember what is spoken in the book of Acts. Acts 2:42 says, "And they continued steadfastly in the teaching and the fellowship of the apostles, in the breaking of bread and the prayers." Verse 41 speaks of baptism, and verse 42 says that they continued in the teaching and the fellowship of the apostles. Please remember that the apostles gave teaching and fellowship immediately after the church had three thousand people saved. Hence, the edification of the new believers is a very crucial matter. What the apostles were doing there is what we are doing here today. The so-called edification of the new believers is the teaching and the fellowship of the apostles. Today you cannot say that once a new believer is saved, you can indifferently let him go. You must give him teaching and tell him to continue steadfastly in this teaching.

The gospel preaching meeting brings the new believers in. After this we need to raise them up. If we have begotten so many and are not able to raise them up, the church will never be strong. Therefore, the gospel preaching must be strong and the new believers' edification must also be strong. Both must be strong in order that we may have a future.

THE MEETING ACCORDING TO 1 CORINTHIANS 14

We all have to learn and wait much before God concerning

how to have this meeting. This meeting is all the brothers and sisters gathering together and some preparing themselves before God to be led to rise up to function. Many people can surely give the church much help when they function. Therefore, in this meeting you can have personal testimonies, sharing, and more than one brother speaking.

The Responsible Brothers
Taking Care of This Meeting

We have to seek out saints who are especially helpful to the brothers and sisters. The responsible brothers need to tell them, "We hope that you can speak more." There are many brothers and sisters who possess no judgment of propriety in their speaking; it is rather clear that they have little gift and little grace. The responsible brothers may inform them privately to speak less. You need to give some people a time limitation, but do not offend the Holy Spirit. If some brothers stand up to speak for only two minutes, they can really render help to the brothers. But they may like to drag on, and when they drag on, their speaking becomes too long. You need to tell such brothers that if they speak for two minutes, the brothers and sisters will receive help, but that the help is reduced by the third minute and exhausted by the fourth minute. Therefore, you must bring them to see that they should speak in a simple way for two minutes. You need to tell some people that it is sufficient for them to speak for five minutes. If everyone who stands up to speak is dealt with thoroughly, this meeting will be strong.

Many people are very self-confident, always believing that they can help others. They do not know that they must touch man's spirit, and they think that they can render help to people. If no one tells them this, they will not know. Therefore, the responsible brothers need to tell them that their words should be brief when they speak before God; when their words are lengthy, they cannot give people help. If the responsible brothers would speak in this way, that would help them. If a certain brother speaks and gives help to people, the responsible brothers should encourage him to speak again. Although the responsible brothers are not all ministers of the word, the care of the church is their business. Therefore, you should not be loose. Encourage some brothers to speak more that the church may receive the supply. You need to restrain some other brothers. When they speak briefly, the church can receive the benefit, but when they speak too long, there is no help.

If the responsible brothers are not passive but active to take care of the meeting, I believe that the type of meeting in 1 Corinthians 14 can bring many riches to us.

The crucial point is that the responsible brothers should not speak loosely or deal with people carelessly. If they are not careful, they will offend the Holy Spirit. As an elder of the church, the most feared thing is to offend the Holy Spirit. The Holy Spirit is the true representative of Christ to execute His authority on earth. The elders must understand the mind of Christ and then speak. If they do not know the mind of Christ, they should not speak. If they do not speak carefully, they will offend the Holy Spirit.

The Sisters Giving Testimonies

Question: In the type of meeting according to 1 Corinthians 14, can the sisters give testimonies?

Answer: I personally think that testimonies may be all right.

Question: According to 1 Corinthians 14, they should not open their mouth.

Answer: Yes, according to 1 Corinthians 14 they should not open their mouth. However, if a sister wants to give a testimony, it would be better for a responsible brother to ask her. This is a different matter, and the responsibility is on the responsible brothers. Her head is covered, and she is not presuming headship.

THE PRAYER MEETING

There are two or three special matters in the prayer meeting which the brothers should pay attention to.

Be Short

First, tell all the brothers who pray to learn to be short.

Ten out of ten prayer meetings are ruined by long prayers.
In the prayer meeting everyone should learn to pray in a short
way. The elderly brothers may have a few long prayers. But
tell the new believers from the very beginning to learn to be
short. For the prayer meeting to have power and be strong,
the prayer has to be short. Long prayers are often padded
with many empty words. When you come to a prayer meeting,
you should remember to tell the brothers to pray short prayers.

Be Genuine

Second, we must warn the brothers and sisters that the
words of their prayer in the prayer meeting must be honest.
Warn the brothers and sisters that their prayer in their own
personal prayer time and their prayer in the prayer meeting
should not differ too greatly. Learn to be real. It is true that
the words uttered in the prayer meeting need to be clear.
When you are having your personal time before God, you may
stop before a sentence is fully uttered; of course, you would
have to continue this sentence in the prayer meeting.
However, there are times when the words you use in the
prayer meeting are not the words you use in your personal
time of prayer. Many prayers in the prayer meeting are indeed
not genuine. Sometimes when you are in a prayer meeting,
you do not know whether a certain brother is praying for you
or for God to hear. Whenever some people pray, they give the
impression that they are praying for man to hear. Therefore,
we need to charge them to pray from their heart; they must
pray for God to hear. Do not let some brothers or sisters make
prayer a kind of preaching of the truth nor let them give an
intelligence report to God. Charge the brothers to learn to
pray short prayers and to pray genuinely. These are the basic
requirements of a prayer meeting. Speak only the words that
you have. Do not go beyond what is genuine.

The Topic Needing to Be Focused

Third, those who are caring for the church in various
localities must make a decision concerning the topics of prayer
in the prayer meeting. We need to learn to do this one thing:
Never allow the brothers to pray as they see fit. We have

seen this in our prayer meetings for twenty years, perhaps close to thirty years. As a result, our prayer meetings are almost powerless. In a prayer meeting with twenty or thirty topics, with each topic being prayed by a different person, the one accord mentioned in Matthew 18 is nonexistent. Without the one accord, how could God listen?

Therefore, the prayer meeting in various localities must also be completely changed. The items for prayer need to be determined, but not necessarily determined beforehand. However, on the night of prayer you need to mention these items. Perhaps you would pray only for one item in one prayer meeting. For example, there might be problems in a locality, and we would pray just for that one locality. In our prayer there must be only one matter, and we must ask all the brothers and sisters to lay aside everything else and pray for this one matter. From beginning to end, the church should pray for this one matter, with everyone bringing this matter to God. A real prayer meeting will be like this.

A prayer meeting does not mean that everyone brings the prayer in his home into the meeting place to pray. In a prayer meeting we must pray specifically with one accord. The responsible brothers should say, "Today we must pray specifically for this one matter." Everyone then prays for this one matter.

If there are five or six items to pray for and a responsible brother stands up to announce them, he should announce one item first. He may say, "We have several matters to pray for; however, we will pray for this one item first." Do not mention other matters. After three or five prayers, you have to see whether the burden is discharged or not. If you feel that you should still pray for that matter, let them continue to pray. If the burden is gone, while the brothers are still sitting there or kneeling, a responsible brother should announce another item. Then the prayers of all the brothers and sisters will be on this topic. After five, ten, or twenty minutes, it may seem that the burden is gone again, and that no one has anything more to pray. The responsible brother should then stand up again and say that there are still a third and a fourth item which need prayer. Do you see? The topic must be focused.

Even if there are three or four topics, they should not be announced at one time. Wait until the first topic has been thoroughly prayed for; then announce the second topic. In this way you will be able to make all the brothers and sisters pray for one item. After the first topic is over, bring in the second; after the second is over, bring in the third. Therefore, in the meeting the responsible brothers should learn before God to guide this meeting. The spirit of the responsible brothers must be open and sensitive. One responsible brother may say, "The prayer for this matter can stop here. There is no need to drag it on any longer." Perhaps there are times when you still need to continue praying. At any rate, after the first matter is finished, the second matter can be brought in. If the burden is finished, you should then rise up immediately to announce the next item.

Sometimes during the entire meeting we can pray only for one matter, perhaps just for a sick brother. At other times we may pray only for the sick ones the entire night. At still other times we may pray for all the unemployed brothers or for just one unemployed brother. Always pray with a focus so that God's children can pray with one accord. I think that this is a very crucial matter. Many prayer meetings are not strong because there are too many topics.

THE BREAD-BREAKING MEETING

The Real Worship Service

The bread-breaking meeting is already quite clear among us, but we must always tell the brothers in various localities to take note that the bread-breaking meeting is the real worship service, the real worship.

Divided into Two Sections

In this meeting we need to see that the first section is always toward the Lord and the second section toward God. In the first section we see the One who was sent; in the second section we come to the One who sent. In the first section we always meet the Lord, and in the second section we meet God. Spontaneously, when these two sections are joined together, the bread-breaking meeting is on the mark.

The First Section Needing to Be Quick

Brothers and sisters, the first section of the bread-breaking meeting must be quick. If your appreciation for the Lord Jesus comes slowly, there will not be enough time. Therefore, if the first section is slow, there will not be enough time for the next section. You must touch the Lord in a quick way during the first section. Perhaps there should not be too many hymns or too many prayers. As soon as you touch the Lord, begin to break the bread. After you break the bread, immediately come before God. I am afraid the problem today is that we begin to break the bread too late.

Perhaps I can say it in this way. Many times you may feel that before God the brothers have already reached the climax of their feelings toward the Lord, yet they have not broken the bread. Therefore, the meeting goes down. After a while a high point is reached the second time, and they still do not break the bread. The meeting goes down again. Perhaps not until a high point is reached a third time do they break the bread. In principle you should break the bread when you reach the high point the first time. If you break the bread when you reach the high point the first time, you will have time to worship God later.

The Need for the Burdens to Be Discharged

The principle of two or three persons in 1 Corinthians 14 is the principle of speaking the word, not the principle of prayer. If we limit the time and the number of people for prayer, I am afraid that some burdens may remain. I am afraid that if the burdens are not discharged after a while, people will go home with their burdens still heavy. This is because when people come to the bread-breaking meeting in the Lord's presence, there are many burdens to be discharged, and if we limit the time and the number of people, their burden will not be discharged, and the burdens of the church will not be discharged either.

I have much feeling concerning this matter. Very often we

have not broken the bread when we have reached a high point. We break the bread after we have climbed to the top two or three times. This is indeed too late. The moment that we reach the high point is always the time to break the bread. Perhaps after a few prayers or hymns, we have already reached the high point. We should then break the bread. Then there will be sufficient time for the worship of the Father.

The Lord Leading Us to Worship Together

The brothers must see that during the time for the Father, the Lord's position is not the same as it was in the first section. At this time, the Lord begins to lead us to sing hymns. It is the Lord who leads us to approach the Father together. It is the Lord who leads us to sing hymns of praise to the Father together. The Son Himself is involved, and He and the many sons praise together. During the second section it is always the case that the children of God together with the Lord Jesus come before God to worship Him. The meeting should reach such a level.

THE SISTERS' MEETING

The sisters' meeting is also a meeting to help the church. There is the need for this meeting in some places, but perhaps there is not the need in other places. At any rate, the sisters' meeting is arranged in the following way:

Giving Opportunity for the Ones Who Have Received Burdens to Exercise Their Gifts

If one or two sisters who have received burdens from the Lord come to a certain place, we should arrange a sisters' meeting for them so that they may have the opportunity to exercise their gifts among the sisters. If there are sisters in the churches in various localities whom the Lord uses and burdens, we will set up a sisters' meeting. If there are no such sisters, then we do not need to set up a sisters' meeting. Since that need is due to certain sisters being used by God, we need to make arrangements for them so that they may have the opportunity to supply the sisters. Otherwise, there is not this kind of need.

Teaching Illiterate Sisters How to Read

There are other sisters' meetings, especially in the countryside, whose nature is different. Some sisters are illiterate and are not able to read the Bible. Teach them to read. This also counts as an aspect of the work, an aspect in helping and caring for those who have already believed in the Lord. For example, among the new believing brothers and sisters, find out who are illiterate and teach them to read. Perhaps in every locality we should make arrangements to teach those who are illiterate to read so that they can read the Bible. Do not let go of this matter by any means. However, this is not an official meeting of the church; rather, this is a work done when the church is serving and preaching the gospel. This is also a part of the Levitical service for the new believers. This is especially for the brothers and sisters to learn to read and to be able to read the Bible.

THE CHILDREN'S MEETING

The children's meeting is also needed. This is also a meeting of the local church in the aspect of the work.

We have children's meetings in various localities. This requires that a few brothers and sisters specifically come forth to do this work. Sisters are perhaps more appropriate. I do not know what materials they are now using in various localities.

In some places they use the Bible to teach the children to read and to memorize. The songs that they sing are composed from Bible verses. They also use pictures.

As to pictures, take heed that this does not lead to deviations. Using pictures of the Lord Jesus is especially inappropriate. Pictures of flowers and birds do not present any problems.

Perhaps there are brothers and sisters among us who are especially experienced with and burdened for the children. They should come forth and give us some materials that the children in various localities may receive the benefit. Perhaps there are already some brothers who are preparing songs for the children.

If the children's meeting is carried out properly, it will also provide a good opportunity for more people to believe in the Lord. This meeting indeed needs to be strong. In the future I hope that there will be a few brothers and sisters who will come forth to prepare some materials for the brothers to take care of the children. When the number of saved ones in various localities increases, spontaneously the children's meeting becomes very crucial, because they are our next generation.

CHAPTER SIX

THE AFFAIRS OF THE SERVICE OFFICE

Scripture Reading:

"And they sold their properties and possessions and divided them to all, as anyone had need" (Acts 2:45).

"For neither was anyone among them in need; for as many as were owners of lands or of houses sold them and brought the proceeds of the things which were sold and placed them at the feet of the apostles; and it was distributed to each, as anyone had need" (Acts 4:34-35).

"And in these days, as the disciples were multiplying in number, a murmuring of the Hellenists against the Hebrews occurred, because their widows were being overlooked in the daily dispensing" (Acts 6:1).

"Let a widow be enrolled, not under sixty years old, having . been the wife of one man" (1 Tim. 5:9).

Today we want to come to the sixth matter, that is, the affairs of the service office—the church business office or work office.

THE BIBLE RECORDING THE ARRANGEMENT
OF THE SPIRITUAL ASPECT OF THE CHURCH IN DETAIL
AND THAT OF THE PRACTICAL AFFAIRS NOT IN DETAIL

In the New Testament it is quite amazing that the arrangement concerning the spiritual aspect of the church is shown in a very detailed and complete way. Concerning the arrangement of practical affairs, however, the Bible tells us only that there was such an arrangement. It does not tell us how the practical affairs were arranged. The Bible speaks in great detail regarding how the spiritual gifts should operate, how the meetings should be conducted, and how the goal of the meetings should be for the building up. It is also sufficiently clear how the church is organized and how the church is local and has brothers, deacons, and elders. It is also quite clear how these elders, who are the overseers, should behave in the church. This time we have seen that the work is also regional. Within a region there are apostles being sent out by God to work and later returning to their own center of work. It is also very clear that there are apostles who take care of the affairs of the church in that region. The Bible, regarding spiritual things, has given us very clear guidance. If any person before God is sufficiently simple, sufficiently pure, sufficiently careful, and willing to learn, then he will not have much problem in understanding the ordination of God; he can obtain clear light.

THE BIBLE HAVING NO DETAILED RECORD OF ARRANGEMENT OF PRACTICAL AFFAIRS

In the New Testament one peculiar thing we repeatedly see is that the church needs a great many arrangements, yet the Bible does not spend much time speaking of the arrangements of practical affairs. It is very reluctant to mention these things.

Today I especially want to read the three portions in Acts. Two passages tell us that we should distribute to people according to each one's need; one passage tells us that a few widows, the Hellenist sisters, were overlooked. The church in Jerusalem at that time had tens of thousands of people, but today you read only these few words: "Distributed to each, as anyone had need." You see that it was very simple. But today in Foochow there are only one thousand believers; yet we still are not able to find out everyone's need. In Shanghai there are a little more than one thousand believers, and we still do not know what the actual need of everyone is. At that time in Jerusalem there were tens of thousands of believers, all newly saved. How could the apostles distribute "to each, as anyone had need"? Please remember how much work and arrangements were needed among them. This is not a matter of one or two days, nor a matter of one or two persons, nor a problem of one or two meals; this is everyone's need.

I believe that anyone who has managed practical affairs knows how difficult this is. For instance, this time on the mountain we have only one hundred persons, and already we are aware of the difficulties. We have three or four brothers at the foot of the mountain and two or three brothers up here. They are busy specifically for these one hundred. They still cannot do a perfect job. What would it take to care for over ten thousand people! The Bible simply says, "Distributed to each, as anyone had need." It was a problem to find out how many "each"s were there. It was another problem to find out the needs of these "each"s, and even more of a problem to distribute to their need. Even though there are only seven words here, we do not know how much labor is involved with these seven words, how many problems, how many responsibilities, how many records, how much calculation is in the background, and how many people need to be sent out to do the distribution. However, this is a peculiar thing in the Bible. Although what they were doing may have taken several days to complete or even several months, the Bible simply records it in a few words, as if the thing happened within half an hour. The events on the day of Pentecost were recorded in great detail, but when it comes to distributing "to each, as anyone had need," which is related to the management of practical affairs, the Bible does not give us a detailed record.

LEARNING IN TWO ASPECTS

The Need to Arrange Practical Affairs

Therefore, today I want the brothers to learn something here, because there is a basic principle. We have to learn to see that there are two aspects. On the one hand, the Bible clearly shows us that arrangements are needed for practical affairs. There may be brothers among us who misunderstand to the point that they think that practical affairs need no arrangements. They seem to think that things will take care

of themselves. There is no such thing. The Bible clearly tells
us to distribute to each, as anyone has need. In this there is
arrangement, not careless dividing and careless distributing.
It is distributing to each, as anyone has need. Therefore,
please remember there are arrangements. There are affairs
that are carried out in a clear and strict way with clear
procedures.

The Persons Being Important, Not the Method

On the other hand, I want the brothers and sisters to take
note that God does not emphasize these arrangements. God
has arrangements, but God did not record all these arrangements in the Bible. The fact that there are arrangements is
spoken of in the Bible, but the method of arrangements is
not recorded. God does not recognize that the method of the
arrangements is important enough to need to be recorded in
the Bible. Perhaps you will ask why. I would like you to know
that there is the need of people who have the wisdom and
the spiritual way before God to be able to obtain the spiritual
wisdom from above. If a person is one who can receive God's
grace, he will receive grace even when he is handling practical
affairs. If a person is one who is filled with the Holy Spirit,
he will know how to carry out spiritual affairs; he will also
be a skillful worker to build up God's tabernacle. This is also
a spiritual work. Therefore, God wants us to pay attention
to learning spiritual matters. From the beginning to the end
of the Bible you can see spiritual arrangements and spiritual
principles, but you do not see the arrangement of practical
affairs. It is not that the arrangement of practical affairs
does not exist, but very little is said concerning it. The fact
is recorded, but not the method.

The Danger of Recording Methods

God knows the temptations and the dangers that are in
man. After a period of time what is spiritual is lost, but a
whole set of business procedures still remains. There can be
such a situation with us that the method of taking care of
things is of God, but the person who carries it out may not

be a spiritual person. If the rules, the details, and the methods by which the apostles took care of practical affairs were clearly laid before us, the readers of the Bible would love to learn these methods first and would not learn to be spiritual first. Because man is of the flesh, man would rather learn what is of the flesh than learn what is spiritual. When many brothers hear about baptism, they argue whether baptism is by immersion into water or by sprinkling. Only afterwards do they pay attention to what the spiritual significance is. Man does not pay attention to the significance of baptism; he argues first about the outward method and circumstance. This is man's nature. Therefore, if there were a handbook for carrying out practical matters in the Bible, I am afraid that the twenty-seven books of the New Testament would be cast aside and this handbook would be the book everyone would have to read. This handbook would gain the attention of the church and would have gained the attention of Christians throughout all the centuries. Therefore, in the Bible there is this characteristic: God shows us only His grace but not His methods for doing things.

There are many churches that have published such handbooks. You may have seen in church history that every time God had a revival, He gained many people, and He used one or a few servants to raise up a group of people. After some days they realized that the church needed some arrangement concerning practical affairs. Therefore, they made many arrangements for church affairs. For fear that they might forget about these arrangements, they recorded them, kept the records, and used them as procedures for doing things so that they could have rules to follow. After some time the spiritual blessing leaked out, the living water was lost, and the power was gone. The second generation could not match the first, the third generation could not match the second, and the spiritual blessing almost completely leaked out; however, the procedures for doing things still remained. This has been the situation of Protestantism.

Therefore, in the Bible we see that God does not tell us the methods for doing things; rather, He left the methods for doing things to the guidance of the Holy Spirit, to the filling of the Holy Spirit, and to the Holy Spirit Himself giving wisdom. This was to avoid a day when the shell would be present, the methods would be present, the procedures would be present, but the blessing would be gone, the living water would be gone, and the spiritual power would be gone. This is a fundamental problem. In church history a method comes out when a group of people are raised up. Yet only the method remains by the time of the second, third, and fourth generation.

For this reason, we have avoided having a method all these years. We do not want a method among us. If the spiritual power is there, if the spiritual life is there, and if we always have the Lord's blessing, then maintaining a method is appropriate. If one day all these spiritual things leak out and all that remains is a method, then that will be like the situation that has existed in Protestantism for so many years. All that remains is an empty frame with all of the inward spiritual things having leaked out. Therefore, we never want a method to come out.

Not Going to the Other Extreme

However, today we cannot go to the other extreme. Many people do so, thinking that there is absolutely no method in the church. I want you to pay attention to this one thing. You are people who study the Bible. You need to see that there are definitely methods in the Bible. Just look at the arrangement at the time of Pentecost. You will see that there was definitely a method to carry out affairs. Frankly speaking, even if you had only one or two thousand people, you would be unable to deal with the situation. If you were like the apostles with over ten thousand people, there would be total confusion. We see that the record of the Bible, however, only touches the matter lightly and then goes on. There are not too many words, but just one phrase: "Distributed to each, as anyone had need." It seems very simple. Behind these few words, however, much work was done. Therefore, I want you brothers to be able to see that during the time of the apostles there were methods for doing things in the churches. But God did not want to leave these methods for later generations to imitate. If God's Spirit is working in a certain place, a method for doing things will naturally come out. If the Lord blesses greatly on a certain occasion, a method will come out spontaneously. When the spiritual blessing dies out, the method for doing things will die out with it. We have no desire that the days of the methods for doing things would be even one day longer than the days of blessing.

We hope, brothers, that you will find a way between these two extremes. There are groups of people, such as the Protestants, who always pay attention to the method. Please remember that the less water a glass has, the more people examine the exterior of the glass. When the glass is no longer used to hold water, it is hung up on the wall as an antique. People always pay attention to external things. We know that God does not allow such things to remain. However, it is not that there are no methods. Chapter six of Acts shows us very clearly that since the problem of a few widows of the Hellenists was not solved, the apostles felt that this matter was not taken care of properly. There were only a few widows who had an unresolved problem among more than ten thousand people. Yet the apostles were not satisfied.

Remember the words that Paul spoke to Timothy. It seems that Timothy recorded the names of the widows in a record book. But in the Bible you cannot find out what a widow's book is. It was mentioned in a casual way. It seems that Timothy was very familiar with this record book. Paul did not say to set up a record book of a certain size, nor did he say how to fill it in. He did not say any of this. He only spoke of enrolling the widows. This means that at that time everyone knew about this way. Later, he simply said not to enroll anyone in a careless way. A problem was discovered— only those sixty years old and above should be enrolled—and the matter was thus settled. He did not say where this record book came from or where it should go.

Prayer Being Needed
concerning How to Carry Things Out

I do not know whether you know this way. In the Bible

there are arrangements and there is a record book, but the Bible does not emphasize the details related to this record book. God does not want to spend the effort to speak even two more sentences about it. What is there is sufficient for us when we need to carry out some affairs. There is a principle that there is the need for a record book. The principle of a record book is here, but as to the way of setting up this record book, you and I need to pray: "Lord, we know that in the early church there was a record book, but we do not know how to set it up. Lord, teach us how to do it." We know that there are arrangements in the church on the one hand, and we need to endeavor before God to find the way on the other hand. God is not willing to lay out before us in the Bible a detailed form of a record book that we can conveniently use to know how to do the work so that we do not need to pray at all. Please remember that God is not willing to do this.

Brothers, I want you to see this before God. Do not pay attention to the method for doing things, because that is dead. Once you pay attention to the method, you will make things dull and deadened. The methods will be set up in such a strong way that one day, when the spiritual blessing is lost, the empty frame of a corpse will still remain. Neither do I want the brothers and sisters to be careless, not expending even a little effort to find out how to take care of affairs, nor ever considering a way to do things in the church. This is also wrong. The Bible does not tell us how to work, but there is a principle in doing things. Today we need to seek out that way. It is not that God does not have a way; God does have a way. Let us be careful never to be so spiritual that we do not have any methods at all. There was still a method there—"Distributed to each, as anyone had need." We still need to carry this out.

THE METHODS THAT WE SEE TODAY

The Need for a Service Office

If there were only seven or eight believers in a local church or if there were only two or three gathered into the name of the Lord, we would not need a business office. If there are a good number of saints in a locality, one hundred, several hundred, or more than a thousand, it would be difficult and confusing without a business office. This is the first problem. Today we want to see something regarding the methods the apostles used to do things in their time.

The Principle of the Record Book

From my point of view, the second thing that I want to specifically point out is the principle of the record book. This is the principle of the widows being enrolled in the record book. If the record book were a method instead of a principle, then God would have told us the length and the thickness of it and its format. But God described the record book in a very brief way. Therefore, you are able to know that there is a principle of the record book. If anything in God's Word is described with only one phrase without any details, then you know that that matter is a principle in the Bible and is, therefore, not in detail.

Man's Memory Not Reliable

Why do we need a record book? We need it because man's memory is not reliable. People depend on their memory to do things. If a person's memory is not reliable, he will not be able to do things. If he sometimes remembers and sometimes forgets, what shall he do in order to carry out anything? Of course, I recognize that some brothers and sisters among us have very good memories. But if one day your memory were faulty, what would you do? What is recorded in the record book is likely to be more accurate than what is in your memory.

Not Easy to Find People

Furthermore, even if one's memory is good, it may be difficult to find him. The one who is taking care of this matter may remember everything, but if he has gone away, what shall we do? If there were a record book, we could open it and read and understand the situation. When Timothy was in the church in Ephesus, he had to take care of the churches in the surrounding area, establishing elders to take care of them. When Timothy went to Rome and Titus went to Jerusalem, what would have been done concerning the problems of the widows if there had been no record books? Maybe they would have had to send a person to Rome to ask Timothy. If Timothy had said, "I have forgotten what I did. I do not know whether I moved one from Pergamos to here or one from Thyatira to there. I have forgotten." Then what would have been done? If record books were there, no one would need to remember, and anyone could open them up.

Therefore, we need to see that church records and the keeping of records in the church are important. This is the principle of the record book. You cannot say that you or I will remember. The whole point is to write it down. It does not matter who it is; once time passes, even the one with the best memory can forget. In the world there are not that many people who can still remember things accurately after many years have passed. Even if you can remember, if suddenly you cannot be found, what shall we do? Therefore, the principle of having the record book comes in. The New Testament does not show us how to write things down in this record book or what kind of records we should keep, but the Lord has shown us that keeping records should be our principle. Therefore, many church matters need to be recorded in a good way.

For this reason, we hope that any church with a considerable number of people would have a business office. If you do not want to use this name, there is no problem. You can call it whatever name you choose. In Shanghai it is called the service office because deacons are the ones taking care of affairs there all the time. We want to keep this principle. We do not want to be like many Protestants who pay attention to these titles; we only want to do things according to the principle. In the church it is acceptable to call it the service office or the business office. The business office is a secular term; the service office is a name given by us.

THINGS HANDLED IN THE SERVICE OFFICE

For Contacting One Another

In this office the main work is to do two things. One is

to meet the need of the brothers and sisters who wish to discuss matters face to face. In a local church there is not much problem if there are not many brothers and sisters. If a church is in a large city or the number of brothers and sisters is more than several hundred, it is not easy to find someone. If someone comes from out of town, he would not know whom to look for. Therefore, the deacons in the church should come to the business office to work. There must be a place, and there must be someone available so that when people come, you have a way to make arrangements to take care of them. You should distribute to each, as anyone has need. You should have a place to keep records, knowing what the needs are, how many people there are, how many family units there are, and how many children there are. There should always be someone supervising and arranging. In other words there must be a place for making arrangements and for contacting one another in order to take care of matters. This is the first use of the service office: mutual contact of one another. Otherwise, if some brother or sister comes to that church to look for other brothers and sisters, he would not know where to go to look for them. There must be a place where he can find them. I do not know if you have seen this principle or not. Such contact with one another requires a business office, or we might call it the service office.

For Keeping Many Records

The second use of the service office is for keeping many records. There are a considerable number of affairs in the church. Every week there are quite a few letters of recommendation written and sent out, quite a few announcements to be made, quite a few things to pray for, quite a few people to be received, and quite a few people baptized. All these things need to be recorded. There may be brothers and sisters who have moved; there may be some who are sick and some who have family problems. It will not work to have one or two persons trying to remember all these things. Even if you could remember all this, when anyone needed to check the information, he would have to look for you, but even so, he could not look into your mind. People need something that they can open up and look into.

I do not mean that these things need to be kept forever. I hope that when the spiritual aspects are gone, these things will be gone too. When there are blessings, these things and these methods are needed. When the blessing is gone, there will be no need for these methods to exist. However, as long as there is blessing, before God we need to seek a way for an arrangement to be made to meet the need. There is a need for a place, for someone to serve, and for the records to be available. This place is our business office. Both the place and the personnel must be available; then it will be possible for all the affairs to be handled. Someone needs to be there to receive people. The records need to be readily available. There should be no need to ask a certain brother for information, for man's memory is not reliable, and man's life is not reliable either. Having records available is more stable and more reliable.

I want the brothers and sisters to understand why we need to have the service office. For what purpose have we had a service office in Shanghai since 1938? The service office meets the local needs and is able to take good care of the affairs of the brothers and sisters. If you do not intend to take good care of the affairs of the saints, then you do not need an office. If you remember, you remember; if you do not remember, you just let it go. That is easy. If, however, you want everything to be well taken care of, you must have the service office.

THE NEED FOR THE SERVICE OFFICE

For this reason we need a training; we need some knowledge concerning this matter. Therefore, I hope that in all the places, although we do not need to be in absolute uniformity, our procedures would be somewhat similar. I believe that the needs among us are similar. Bear in mind that what we should do will be according to the principle of Acts 2 through 6, according to the principle of the record book. We ask God to give us a method which will match our need. In the Bible there is a method to take care of things, but the Bible does not pass it on. So we also do not expect to pass on our method. Those in the beginning had a need; therefore, they sought out a method. Presently, a few of our brothers have found a suitable method. Perhaps there will be a new method, another method, after five or ten years to meet the need of that time.

The Need for a Room to Receive People

Since there is such a need, there is a place, which we temporarily call the service office. At least in this place we can put a few tables and a few shelves. The place needs to be large enough to accommodate those who are looking for others. We should be able to receive people and handle all the affairs. This place can be either near the meeting place or within the meeting hall.

The Need for People to Work in the Office

Second, there is a need for people to be in the office, especially a group of deacons, to learn to take care of others. Of course, it is good for some brothers and sisters to come and help, but it is best to let the deacons bear the responsibility.

Brothers and Sisters Taking Turns to Work

It would be very easy for the church to use the funds from the offering box to hire people to work for the whole day, but I feel that this is not the church. If the church can spend money to hire Levites, it can also spend money to hire priests. This would restore the system of salaries. I hope that the work of the Levites and the priests would be done without pay and by brothers and sisters who take turns. Therefore, it is the same with the work in the business office. (Forgive me for using the word *business,* which is a secular term.) I would like for the brothers and sisters to separate some time during the week to put themselves into this kind of Levitical work. One brother may be willing to give one day. Another brother may be willing to give two days, an hour, or two hours. In this way there will be brothers and sisters taking care of the practical affairs in the office.

For Notification and Inquiry

One brother may want to notify us that another brother is sick. He only needs to come to the service office, and the deacons can immediately notify the responsible brothers or other brothers. Perhaps after a short time, the service office can send out this information. The service office should always have a set of pre-addressed envelopes. Whenever something happens, they can prepare copies of the information either by mimeograph or by hand and immediately mail them out. As soon as something occurs, the brothers and sisters throughout the whole city could be informed within one or two hours. Whenever they have time in the service office, they should address the envelopes and prepare them for later use. We are not copying the methods of the world, but we have to take care of affairs.

For example, during the past ten years or more in Shanghai, if you did not know where a brother resided, you could telephone the service office. All that is needed is to check the card file. Perhaps that brother went to Nanking and would not return for one or two days. If there had been no service office, it would not have been easy for you to find him. We are not copying the ways of the world; we want God's children to know how to handle affairs.

In another case someone may go to another locality. The church in that locality may write to ask if that person was baptized in our midst as he has claimed. If the elder says that he does not know, or that this person seems to have been there before, what can we do? When the number of brothers and sisters increases and the number of baptized ones also increases, there is the need for records. If you have the records, once you look them up, you will find out. This one was baptized on a certain date and met with us for more than two years, but since then we have not seen him. Today this one has been found in another city. We know what his situation was during those two years, but not since then. Now we can ask him: "Since those two years, where have you been? Whom have you met with?" Then there is a way to take care of him and to help him. Things of this sort require records.

Today in a large city like Shanghai or in a place like Foochow, there are district meetings. When anyone comes to ask about the location of the meeting place or about the time when the responsible brothers can be found, someone needs to be available to answer these questions. Therefore, everyone who serves in the business office should know these answers and be able to reply immediately and render help. If there is something the serving one cannot handle, he should refer the matter to the responsible brothers. If the serving one can handle the matter, there is no need to look for the responsible brothers. Otherwise, the responsible brothers would need to receive people all day long, and they would not have any way to get anything done. Many things need to pass through the hands of the deacons, and from the hands of the deacons to the hands of the responsible brothers or to their homes.

I thank God that during the time of the apostles, they handled their affairs well. We can see this because the apostles heard the murmurings concerning the Hellenist widows. It was the duty of the brothers and sisters who were deacons and deaconesses to have their eyes open. Once something happened, they notified the responsible brothers. Then, as you can see, Peter immediately took action. Therefore, in order to take good care of a church, it is not as complicated before God as we think, like Protestantism is. Neither is it as simple as we think. Protestantism has too much organization, but we have overthrown the biblical organization. Both are wrong. Therefore, we need to have a place to conduct business.

For Receiving Others, Caring for Others, and Speaking the Word

Next, we need to have someone there to receive people every day. From morning to evening, if anyone comes to ask about something, there should always be someone there to answer. Therefore, you need to tell the local brothers and sisters to serve not only in other matters but also in the business office. However, the service office should devote a great deal of time every day to helping the church. From the viewpoint of some people, this is not spiritual. We can answer by saying that David said that he would rather be a doorkeeper in God's temple. We should not be spiritual to such an extent that we could not keep the door of the Holy of Holies well. Do not consider that the Levites and the priests are different. Both are important! Without the Levitical service, there is no church. May we all have a heart to serve two or three hours in the church taking care of God's affairs, serving God, and serving His people so that the entire Body will go forward. Never make the work your own work. We need the entire Body to work there and to learn there. Therefore, we need brothers and sisters to come and be on duty to take care of the affairs.

There are many church affairs that require face to face discussion. For example, how do we make arrangements for brothers from out of town? Some brothers coming to your place do not know the way, so you have to pick them up. Or how should you take care of orphans and widows who are passing through your place? There may be some people coming to your place to look for certain brothers and sisters, but because they do not know their way, they need deacons to help them. There are many things that the church needs to do. Seek out some who have the time to help those in need. Often there are accidents, family problems, and sicknesses. The church should be notified of these things immediately. The brothers who are deacons need to find brothers at once who can help these ones.

Some people find their way to the church meeting place to hear a message, and there are many who knock on the door and want to come in to hear the gospel. You cannot say that the owner is not home, that you do not know how to speak, or that you are a servant. When people come to the door, either you yourself take care of him or find a brother to come right away to preach to him. In the future, if God grants us grace and we distribute tracts in an adequate way, many people will come knocking on the door of the meeting hall to hear the gospel as a result. You cannot say it is not yet time for the meeting. You need to speak to them, or perhaps ask them to take a seat while you find another person to come to speak to them. It will happen very naturally that people will want to hear the gospel. Therefore, I hope you will pay attention to this service office; you need a place and you need deacons.

For Recording Various Works and Keeping a Name List

Third, you need to always remember the principle of the record book. The deacon on duty needs to record all of the matters in the business office, with the exception of things that happen incidentally or things that still need to be carried out. In other words, except for the slips of paper underneath the glass on the table, the rest of the matters, which are those that have already been carried out and are finished, need to be recorded. The procedure that was used to carry these things out should be written down, and the record kept there. In this way, when the need arises to check the facts, they can be known. These records are very important. All of the people baptized in a meeting must be recorded. All of the people received in a meeting must be recorded. All of the people who have had hands laid on them in a meeting must be recorded. All of the letters of recommendation sent out from a meeting must be recorded. Furthermore, copies of all the letters of recommendation must be kept on file. In every meeting place there must be a record of the names of all the brothers and sisters, their address, age, date of salvation, and any other important information, such as the date of their spiritual turns or their present spiritual condition. Everything must be written down completely. All those who have signed their names in the gospel meetings need to be recorded. You need to have the new believers go to visit those who came to the gospel meetings. Whatever number of people came to hear the gospel, that many new believers are needed to go and visit them and care for them. These new believers need just as many older believers to care for them as well. These new believers are there, one generation after another. You need to record their affairs in detail. Through this you will know the present situation of those who are being cared for by the ones whom you have sent. The arrangement of the work of the priests also needs to be recorded. We assign them one by one. How many are placed in this work and how many are placed in that work are all recorded at the same time.

The Responsible Brothers
Using the Records for Oversight

Not every brother and sister will keep good records. In the beginning there will be things that are overlooked, and there will be difficulties. You need to check the books to see who has been overlooked. As soon as you check, you will know by whom a certain person is being cared for or why he has not been cared for. Whether this job is done well or not depends on whether or not the worker has a good system. With good records you can follow people closely. The greatest use for records is in following up on people; it is not merely for recordkeeping. Records can keep you informed. If you need to check, you can find out. When someone is about to go to another city and wants to find out about the situation of a certain brother or some spiritual matters about him, they can give him an answer based on the records. In another aspect, a responsible brother can often find out from the record book whether certain brothers or sisters have done what they should have done. The responsible brothers in all the localities need to look up on their cards the names of these people frequently. This is their responsibility.

With all these cards, you can divide and assign certain ones to be responsible for a certain number of people. You have to map out districts to find out who is in this district and who is in another district. As responsible ones, the overseers need to oversee. Your job is to oversee. Often you need to observe and ask, "Brother, have you done this?" "Brother, have you taken care of that matter?" Everywhere you go, you should ask, "What is the situation with the five brothers you have just finished visiting?" "What is the situation with the ten brothers you have just finished visiting? Have you overlooked one and not visited him? During this past week, have you visited all of them?"

All the Brothers Serving Being the Way Today

The responsible brothers should not merely preach a

message once from the podium and then consider the job over. It is your responsibility to motivate the brothers who are with you to work. This is what you need to accomplish; this is the way today. If you do not have this, you have no way. If it were the same as before, with only one message preached per week, then everyone would be a preacher resting six days and working one day. God worked six days and rested one day; today we rest for six days and work one day. No wonder all of the preachers have become lazy! Therefore, every one of you needs to labor every day, and you also have to cause all of the brothers to serve. Brothers, the question is not whether you have done the work, but whether you have done it and have a way to cause others to do it as well.

On the one hand, your job is to do the work yourself, and on the other hand, it is to lay hold of others to do the work and then follow up on them. After you go down the mountain, I will write letters to ask you how many people you oversee in a week. We cannot have an elder who does not oversee. Today if I hire ten laborers to work on the mountain and assign one brother to supervise, I do not expect the supervising brother to pick up a bamboo basket and carry it. I want him to supervise. He should not say, "Not one of the ten would carry it. Therefore, I carried it." If the brother were to say this, he would not be worthy to be a supervisor. He would be useless. We have the ability before God to make sure that others carry the load. We have the ability before God to make them work. If you can cause six or ten brothers to serve, there is the church. Do not complain to us, saying, "Why should we stress this matter?" The reason is that if we do not work in this way, there will be no church. You may go out to preach to two or three people and may continue doing so. True, you have your own work, and I cannot disregard it. Yet you also need to lead other brothers and sisters to do the work. Never go astray from this way. If you do, you are wrong.

We need to bring every brother into this way. In matters pertaining to the gospel, let them preach the gospel and let them share in the care for the gospel. You need to take care of the new believers. You need to lead them to do the work and to take care of practical affairs. Do not turn matters over to them and consider the job done. You need to follow up on them until the work is finished. You need to continue watching over them to see how they are doing. You need to ask, "Do you have any problems? If you do, I am here to help you solve them." In this way, you will see the church come forth.

For the church to come forth, there is the need for people to come forth. The day will come when you see the church serving and the entire church preaching the gospel. Then I would say that God's way of recovery on the earth has begun and then He will have the church on the earth. Otherwise, Christianity has been taken captive to Babylon, and to this day it has not returned. Today there are still those who are passive. Today there are still some who are the mediatorial class—on one side is God and on the other side is man with a mediatorial class in the middle through which people must pass before they can serve. I do not know whether or not you have seen this. This is the whole problem.

The Service Office Being the Instrument
for Carrying Out the Affairs

Therefore, the service office is the instrument with which the brothers take care of affairs. From it you can obtain information and find out about different situations. The deacons and deaconesses have things recorded there. Based on their records, you can see what is the situation of the church today. You can observe the brothers and sisters, oversee them, and tell them what they should do. Tell the lazy ones that they must labor. Tell the proud ones that they should learn humility. Step by step, bring them to be attentive to what they do. Brothers, have you seen what is called the work of God? It is not merely a matter of preaching from the podium. We recognize that we cannot do away with the ministry of the word; this ministry is very precious. But you also have to bring every one of the brothers and sisters to serve. When that time comes we will thank God that He has a way in China.

In the beginning you need to tell the deacons and deaconesses that when the brothers and sisters come to ask questions, they need to be courteous, polite, and not cold when replying. All of these matters are your responsibility. You need to go and carry it out and not let it go by carelessly. You need to be firm and at the same time meek, not letting things go by. You need to learn to serve in these matters; do not be afraid of troubles. You need to tell them, "He who transcribes must transcribe well; he who records must record accurately. If there is a little inaccuracy, you are responsible. Therefore, when the brothers need to retrieve what you have recorded, it will be easy. You should not handle it carelessly. This is God's work." When you handle things in this way, the lazy ones will have to resign. We do not work only six days and rest one day; we work every day, seven days a week. Many people are lazy because they put aside other things and use all of their time to study the Bible. Once you are careless, of course, you have nothing to do. If you mean business before God, you only need to invest an extra hour, and then the church will be built up one day earlier. If you invest an extra hour, pay attention to one more person, ask one more person—today you ask five brothers, and tomorrow you ask ten brothers, "Have you done your job?", then, I tell you, the service of the church will be raised up one day earlier. On the one hand, we need a very good system and we need arrangements, and on the other hand, we need a record book to write everything down. Finally, you who are the responsible ones need to follow up on people. Although there is a business office and a system set up there, if you do not adequately follow up on people to do the work, it is useless. Never be slack; cause them to see that every one of us needs to serve. One day you will see that all of you have a habit of overseeing each other. Affairs should be taken care of properly; there should not be only one brother doing things there. Learn to go on together.

If you are clear about God's purpose, you will bow your head before God and worship Him, saying, "Lord, have a way among us so that You can go on!" You can see that there is only one purpose for all the children of God, that is, to serve Him. Otherwise, there indeed is a problem. May God give us the grace.

NEEDING TO BEGIN WITH CONSECRATION

Question: How do you motivate all the brothers to work?

Answer: I think that this way still has to begin with consecration. This is a new way, and we need to have good arrangements. First, we need to show the brothers that the service is the whole church serving, with every member of the Body having its function. Everyone should be a priest. You need to remind them of this one matter and do so emphatically. You also have to tell them about the matters of authority. I believe that we also need to pay attention to the matter of selling all. If a person does not sell all, his talk of service is false and will not work. There is the need for him to give all he has in order to serve God. Therefore, the basic thought is that everyone needs to offer all in order to serve God. Today God is calling those who belong to Him to come forth and serve Him. Otherwise, everything that we have seen this time will be dead. It will become merely a viewpoint and a method, and you will find it unworkable as a result. Therefore, it is not a matter of method but a matter of God opening up a way for us.

Nevertheless, when we go to speak this matter, we should speak in a strong way. We should not speak in a begging way, as if service is to patronize God and do Him a favor. If we are standing on that ground, we are altogether wrong. We need to let the brothers see that their service to God is a high and glorious thing. Today we should by no means live carelessly on the earth as before, but we must follow the Lord in all things. Therefore, we must be strong. Once we are strong, we will cause others to come forth. We need to tell them, "Today our occupation is something on the side. We must learn to serve God." The way that we take must be straight, and our tone must be right. We should not bring ourselves down to a low level; do not beg people for God. We cannot beg people to believe in God, and even the more, we cannot beg people to serve God. To serve God requires that man come to God to be accepted. Man needs to believe in God by himself. Yet what is this that we beg people to believe in God? Today God wants us to serve Him. We have no choice but to come and serve. We need to be very clear about this before God. We must see accurately. If we see accurately, then others will see accurately. Everyone must serve God; otherwise, there will be no church. When the brothers and sisters fall prostrate before God, when they crawl to come and serve God, then we will see that what we have talked about is not a difficult matter.

USING ONLY THOSE PEOPLE GAINED BY GOD

Question: In a certain locality, not everyone has given up all. Some have given up all, and some still have not. What shall we do about taking care of the practical affairs?

Answer: We cannot use people who have not been gained by God. As many people as God has gained, we will use. We have to be cautious of the rest of the people. We must endeavor to bring them over to God's side. We need to continue working until that happens.

The Need to Labor until Everyone Serves

Our way is to learn to build up. Everyone must have the goal of building up. Therefore, this time we would not relax our requirement for service. They need to put their whole being into it. This word must be spoken clearly. Today all the co-workers need to put everything into this work. We will ask some of the brothers also to put everything into this work. We need to tell them, "This is not something that only a few should do. We are putting everything into this work. You also need to put everything into this work, including your material possessions, your strength, and your life. All that you have needs to be put into this work." Before God, the higher you can climb, the more God will bless you. The more you lower your tone, the fewer people will come. The more afraid you are, the fewer people will come, because God does not bless that attitude. Therefore, you have to put yourself in a right position.

If your position is wrong, people will not come. God will never bless that kind of attitude. It will be quite evident that even your own service is not healthy. Before God you must see that being a servant of God is not a favor to Him, but His favor to you; otherwise, how could you serve God? If someone invites you to participate in a worldly occupation, many would thank that one. Today when people are asked to come to serve God, should they expect God to thank them instead? When you go out to invite people, do you beg them? If so, your standing is wrong.

Please forgive me, there are a few things I have no patience for. If I hear a brother in a certain place say, "Today God loves you and you need to come and serve Him," as if God will be very happy if this one will just come and serve Him, I have no patience for this at all. You need to tell them, "If you serve God, you should be very happy that a person like you can serve Him." Service to God is an opening; you have to go after it. It is not that you are doing God a favor, that you are doing God an honor, and that even intelligent people like you should also come to serve God! Formerly, it was those who could not earn a living who came to be preachers, but now such ones as you should also come! It is an honor to the preaching profession to have a person such as you! I tell you, this attitude is entirely wrong. A Japanese Presbyterian preacher once said that all those who study theology are poor students. However, though he was not a poor student, he went to study theology also. As soon as I heard that, I realized there was no way at all with this man. There is no such thing as a good student doing God a favor by doing His work! When I hear this kind of word, it makes me angry before the Lord.

To Serve God Being Our Glory

We need to see that in our lifetime it is our glory if we can even crawl to God to serve Him. If you consider that God should use a person like you, then you are foolish, very foolish. If God can receive a person such as you, this is the greatest grace and the greatest glory. How strange it is that people would consider that serving God is doing Him a favor! Therefore, I hope that before God you will see that there is nothing more glorious than to serve God. It would even be a glorious thing if I could serve God by standing at the door as a beggar. It is a wonder that God wants us. God said, "I will have mercy on whom I will have mercy." It is His mercy that He wants me to be His servant. Suppose that you are more intelligent than most people, your position is higher than that of most others, your family has a good financial situation, and you did very well in school, and you now become a preacher. In the eyes of most people this would be a very strange thing that you also would come to serve God! Let me tell you that this attitude is altogether wrong.

Therefore, brothers, when you go out this time, you should not exhort people to come and serve God, nor beg them to serve Him. If that happens, this work will be damaged by you; it will be finished. You must have this kind of attitude: If people think that to serve the president is glorious, they need to know what a great difference there is between the president and God. If I can serve God, this is my greatest glory. When man offers things to God, the consideration is not how painful it may be to give up those things; rather, the consideration is whether or not God will accept what you offer. How do you know God will accept it? You need to remember that this is not merely a matter of consecration, but also a matter of being sanctified. You need to show them that the big question is whether or not God will accept their offering. If God accepts it, this is their glory. It is not a matter of whether or not man will offer something; it is a matter of whether or not God will accept it. Therefore, your way before God needs to be straight, you need to keep your position, and you need to stand on God's ground to speak. As soon as you lower your position, you have nothing to say and everything is finished. Forgive me for saying this, but I would even doubt your own service.

Man cannot be proud before God. If a person thinks that it is a waste for someone like him to come out to preach, you can ask him, "Within these ten years, has God used you to do anything? You are a person that God would never use!" What a great glory it is for man to serve Him! We ask God to grant us grace that in the matter of church affairs, we could do well and walk a straight path.

CHAPTER SEVEN

DISTRICT MEETINGS

If the locality of a church is large and also has many saints, district meetings become a necessary arrangement. We do not believe as the Congregationalists do that each congregation is a unit, for that is not the teaching of the Bible. The teaching of the Bible does not allow for taking a congregation as the unit, but a locality as the unit. For example, Corinth was a locality, and Rome was a locality. Therefore, if the number of brothers and sisters in a locality is quite large, as in the case of Jerusalem, which had tens of thousands of believers, you will realize that it is impossible to meet in one place. Moreover, there were already three thousand or five thousand saved in the first few days in Jerusalem; perhaps they were unable to meet in one place within the first few days. Therefore, we see clearly that there must be some kind of arrangement for the meetings.

FIFTY IN A GROUP OR ONE HUNDRED IN A GROUP

We are not taking the following section of the Bible as the basis; we are only taking this section of the Bible as our guide; it leads us and guides us. Remember the occasions when the Lord Jesus fed the five thousand and the four thousand. The Lord could not distribute the bread to the people because of the large number. Spontaneously, the Lord made an arrangement either with fifty in a group or with one hundred in a group. Today we accept the principle of this arrangement of the Lord. When the number of saints is quite large in a certain place, we can learn from the way of the Lord to divide people into groups of fifty or one hundred.

I already mentioned some days ago that the Lord did not always divide the people entirely into groups of fifty or one hundred. The Lord divided some of them into groups of fifty and some into groups of one hundred, meaning that these two numbers were convenient numbers. Therefore, when the number of people in the church becomes large, we need to divide them into groups. This does not mean that we must form a separate meeting when we reach a certain fixed, legal number. Rather, we say that based on convenience, geography, and the size of the congregation, there can be a meeting of about fifty people or perhaps a meeting of about one hundred. The number one hundred is twice as much as fifty; therefore, the Lord was only giving us a convenient number.

Based upon this principle, I think that the responsible brothers in all the localities should learn to make arrangements to have the people divided into districts whenever their number becomes large. The number could be fifty, one hundred, or a little more than one hundred. In any case we should begin to have district meetings when those meetings reach these two numbers. This kind of meeting is most convenient because it is easy to take care of the saints and visit them when the number is small. There is also more opportunity for the saints to function in the meeting when the number is small. Numbers between fifty and one hundred are very good for meeting. They are very convenient in every way.

Meeting Separately in Districts

The gospel preaching meeting as well as the prayer meeting and the new believers' meeting may be carried out in the different districts. If we want to do so, even the edification meeting can be carried out by separate districts. If we wish to combine some meetings together, I think that the edification meeting would be a good one to combine and perhaps the gospel preaching meeting as well. If there are brothers who are workers in this region and if they want to have some message meetings for the brothers and sisters, it is obvious that combining them is more convenient. All the other meetings may be held separately—the prayer meeting, the bread-breaking meeting, and the new believers' meeting. All these may be held in the districts.

Caring for the Saints by Districts

In this way we can care for the saints by districts. If there are meetings by districts in a locality, the responsible brothers should learn to make arrangements so that there will be someone bearing responsibility in every district. The responsible ones in every district should listen to the overseers. The responsible ones need to learn to bear responsibility and to take care of the whole spiritual situation in every district. They should concern themselves with all the work and take care of it. These are their responsibilities.

Having Balanced Growth

If the number of people in any church has increased, the area has been well divided into districts, and there has been adequate caring in each district, then you will see that all the saints will be involved in the meetings. This is because many people will be able to have balanced growth, and they will all be able to pray and fellowship before God. As long as the number is small, there is no need to divide into districts. When the number is large, there is such a need.

MEETING BY DISTRICTS IN JERUSALEM

The Bible does not show us how Jerusalem was divided into districts. When we read the book of Acts, we know that there were districts, although they did not use our terminology. The prayer meetings were in individual homes. When Peter was put into prison, as you recall from the story of Rhoda, the house of Mark was a place of prayer. Let me repeat that the Bible does not give us all the particular detailed items of the affairs of the church, because God is not pleased when everything is structured. However, in the Bible there are some clues concerning the arrangement of all the affairs. These clues are placed in the Bible. This causes the church in every generation to learn to seek God and to make arrangements according to the Lord even though the church encounters the same situations again and again.

According to the actual situation, it would have been impossible for all the brothers and sisters in Jerusalem to meet together to break bread. It would have been impossible in practice. If there had been only one cup, how large should that cup have been? If there had been only one bread, how would you have distributed that bread? How much time would you have needed to spend to pass the bread to several thousand people? Later, the number became tens of thousands. Passing the bread to so many people would be impossible. Even if they took all seven days of the week to meet, it would nevertheless be very hard to distribute the bread and pass the cup in a good way. Therefore, we can see very clearly that they met by districts in those days. The house of Mark was a house among many houses.

Keeping This Principle

Therefore, I hope that we would always keep this principle before God. On the one hand, we acknowledge that the Bible mentions arrangements concerning these matters. On the other hand, we also acknowledge that the Bible does not give us a regulation concerning the arrangement of these matters. In the Bible, God always maintains a principle rather than giving us detailed regulations concerning how outward things should be done.

For example, these days we write letters of recommendation or letters of introduction. In the Bible we see only the letter of recommendation, but the Bible never tells us how this letter should be written. Paul said that he did not need letters of commendation. "Are we beginning again to commend ourselves? Or do we need, as some do, letters of commendation to you or from you?" (2 Cor. 3:1). This tells us that there was a recommendation letter, but we are not told how it was written. Therefore, we are learning year by year to have letters of recommendation and how to write them in a good way. Paul did not leave us a form or a handbook of form letters so that we would only need to fill in the blanks. We should be learning all the time how to write such letters.

When God does things in the church, He always gives just a principle. He only shows you that He is doing something; He never reckons that the Holy Spirit is apart from the church. From God's view the Holy Spirit is in the church to represent Christ; the Holy Spirit dwells in the church. There-fore, as long as we have the principle concerning a certain matter and are willing to submit ourselves to the Head of the church, the Holy Spirit can teach us how to carry it out. I hope that you can see this matter, especially the matter of dividing into districts. Even though we have no details or regulations of the Bible to tell us how to do it, we know that in practice it is impossible not to have meetings by separate districts. Moreover, in the book of Acts we see the principle of meeting by districts. The saints met from house to house. The house of Mark was one of those houses. Acts 2:46 says, "From house to house." This verse shows us the principle of the districts. Today we ask God to teach us how to carry out these things based on the principle in the Bible.

I wish you would remember this principle—the Bible does not keep anything from us regarding spiritual things. It speaks in a very detailed way. However, concerning the aspect of practical affairs, concerning the Levitical service (in matters of serving God, there is service in the nature of the Levites), the Bible gives us only clues, not regulations. It shows us that there are such matters, but it does not show us how these matters are carried out. Today when you are going to carry them out, you will find that the Holy Spirit has not left you, that the Holy Spirit is still in the church, and that Christ is still the Head of the church through the Holy Spirit. In order to know this matter, you can wait and pray. Then you will be able to gain the light. I hope that the brothers will see the matter of meeting by districts and practice according to this principle.

CHAPTER EIGHT

THE ARRANGEMENT
OF THE LOCAL CHURCH
AT THE CENTER OF THE WORK

Another thing we have to consider is what we should do with the local church at the regional center of the work. There are two types of local churches: the general local church and the local church at the regional center of the work. Actually there is not much difference between the two. There is only a small difference related to the place of apostles in that local church.

A LOCAL CHURCH HAVING ELDERS,
DEACONS, AND BROTHERS AND SISTERS

In a place like Philippi, for example, you can see that there were elders, deacons, and brothers and sisters in the church. Philippians 1:1 says very clearly, "To all the saints in Christ Jesus who are in Philippi, with the overseers and deacons." In other words, this letter was written to all the believers, the overseers, and the deacons in the church. This is the arrangement within a general local church: There are overseers, deacons, and brothers and sisters.

AN EXTRA GROUP, THE APOSTLES, BEING
IN THE LOCALITY AT THE CENTER OF THE WORK

It is somewhat different if you are in a local church at the center of the work because there is an extra group, the apostles. In every locality the overseers always administrate the local churches. In the locality where the regional center of the work is, there are the apostles.

The Apostles Also Being Elders

The apostles administrate the work in a certain region.

The apostles are for the work, but at the same time they also administrate the local church there. Therefore, when the apostles are in the locality which is a regional center of the work, they are there as apostles on the one hand and as overseers, elders, on the other hand. The apostles care for the work in a certain region or area. Perhaps the word *region* is too formal. As long as you know what it means, that is good enough; we are not fighting over words. The apostles administrate the work in a certain area, and they also administrate the affairs of the local church at the center of the work.

However, the apostles should not directly administrate a local church in their status as apostles. Therefore, the apostles at the same time become the elders.

The Bible shows us that when the church held a conference to discuss how to handle matters in the church (which only happened once in the Bible), they sent out letters saying, "The apostles and the elder brothers..." in Jerusalem (Acts 15:23).

Here I want to point out to you that Peter was an apostle, even a leader among the apostles. However, Peter was also an elder in Jerusalem. First Peter 5:1 says, "The elders among you I exhort, who am a fellow elder." Please remember that Peter was not only an apostle but also an elder. Second John 1 says, "The elder to..." Third John 1 says, "The elder to..." In 1 Peter 1:1 Peter tells us that he was an apostle. He wrote the Epistle as an apostle, but in 5:1 he shows us that he was also an elder. At the beginning of his second and third Epistles, John said that he was an elder. It is quite peculiar that, unlike Paul or Peter, John does not mention that he was an apostle. At the beginning of each Epistle, Paul shows us that he wrote the Epistle as an apostle, but John, in his second and third Epistles, says in a simple and straightforward way that it was an elder who wrote the Epistles. Therefore, you can see that the two greatest apostles in Jerusalem were also elders in Jerusalem. Peter and John, the two most renowned among the apostles in Jerusalem, were elders in Jerusalem. With the exception of James, there is no record that any of the other apostles in Jerusalem were elders. In the book of Acts, Peter, John, and James are three noted apostles. The Epistles tell us that two of them were elders.

During the conference of the church, James was the one who made the final decision. According to the history of the church and the word of the Bible, we can see that he was an elder in Jerusalem at that time. Furthermore, according to the Bible, James was ahead of Peter, since it was James who decided on matters.

Therefore, in the church where there is a regional center of the work, you can let the local brothers, the dependable, elderly ones who have the spiritual weight, learn to oversee. At the same time, there are workers who are the elders of the local church on the one hand and the apostles in that region on the other hand.

The Apostles Not Dealing with
Matters Directly Concerned with a Local Church

If you are elders, you cannot administrate affairs of other local churches. If you are elders in Jerusalem, you cannot administrate affairs in Samaria. In the Bible elders are always local. You cannot go beyond the sphere of your local church to go to another local church to administrate their affairs. If you are an apostle, you should not directly administrate the affairs of a local church. An apostle can deal with the local elders, but an apostle cannot deal directly with the affairs of a local church.

Let me give you an example. The work in Corinth was carried out by Paul. In Acts we see clearly that Paul went to Corinth and rendered them help. I want you to see that the relationship between Paul and Corinth was close and deep. Paul wrote two letters to the Corinthians. Not only did Paul go to Corinth himself; he even sent others to Corinth, such as Timothy and Titus. Paul did all these things, but there was no way for him to cast out the sinner in Corinth. Paul was an apostle, but he was not an elder in Corinth. Paul could not post an announcement saying that since this one had committed sin, he would remove him. Paul had to say to the church in Corinth, "Remove the evil man from among your-selves" (1 Cor. 5:13). Paul had no way to remove this man for them. Why was this? Paul was an apostle, not an elder. In the Bible Paul did not tell us that he was an elder in a certain locality. Rather, Paul was an apostle to the Gentiles. He could not administrate a local church. The apostle could not directly handle the administration of a local church. The elders can administrate the church in their own locality but not those in other localities. The apostles can administrate the work of the region, but they cannot directly handle the local administration. The affairs of Corinth had to be handled by the Corinthians, not by Paul.

As an apostle, how did Paul deal with the situation in Corinth? He said, "In the name of our Lord Jesus, when you and my spirit have been assembled, with the power of our Lord Jesus, to deliver such a one to Satan for the destruction of his flesh, that his spirit may be saved in the day of the Lord" (vv. 4-5). When you work, you can only use spiritual authority to deliver such a one to Satan, but you have no way to remove him. If the Corinthians would not remove him, Paul had no way to do it. I am not sure if you have seen this. This is the arrangement regarding the church in the Bible.

Peter Having to Bear Two Responsibilities

In Jerusalem, a local church at the center of the work, Peter had to bear two responsibilities. He had to be in Jerusalem taking care of the work in that area, and at the same time, he was also an elder in Jerusalem. If he had not been an elder in Jerusalem, then he would have had no way to directly administrate the affairs of Jerusalem. Peter and John were elders in Jerusalem, and James was also an elder in Jerusalem. I do not have the complete assurance to say that all the apostles who lived in Jerusalem were always elders in Jerusalem. Probably, those whose names were mentioned were all elders in Jerusalem. Peter had to administrate the affairs in Samaria; therefore, Peter was also an apostle. He took care of the work in that area based on his status as an apostle and administrated the church in Jerusalem based on his status as an elder. This matter is very clear in the Bible. Therefore, the many co-workers in the local church at a center of the work today need to be responsible for the work on the one hand, and they may need to be elders on the other hand. You are elders, and at the same time, you may also be apostles, administrating the work in other places. I hope you can see the relationship between these two responsibilities.

One day when Antioch had a problem, they sent some to Jerusalem to inquire about this. When all the brothers in Jerusalem decided to send a letter, they could say to the saints that the apostles and the elders in Jerusalem had made such a decision. As far as the apostles were concerned, this was a regional matter. As far as the elders in Jerusalem were concerned, this was a matter of the local church. The decision was made with apostles and elders. The apostles and elders decided this matter together.

I do not know if you have seen this. I feel this is a beautiful thing. You need to know that in the aspect of the spiritual work of the church, there is not much room left for your imagination, nor much for you to add. God has put this in front of us in a very detailed way: It is the apostles who administrate the work, and it is the elders who administrate the local church. Peter bore both responsibilities at the same time.

Some Apostles Not Being Elders

I still need to point out that there were apostles, such as Paul and Barnabas, who were not elders. According to our understanding, after careful study we cannot find any place in the Bible that tells us that Paul was also an elder. In the church in Antioch, Paul and Barnabas had a part only in the ministry of the word, not in the church affairs. They had a part in the ministry, but they were neither deacons nor elders; they did not hold these offices. They were prophets in Antioch. Therefore, Paul and Barnabas, the two apostles in Antioch, were in the ministry; they did not hold any office in the church.

ANTIOCH BEING ANOTHER BEGINNING
BY THE HOLY SPIRIT

The beginning in Antioch was initiated by the Holy Spirit. Please take note that the beginning in Jerusalem was initiated by the Holy Spirit and that the beginning in Antioch was also initiated by the Holy Spirit. It was not that Antioch thought up a method for going out to work but rather that the Holy Spirit initiated another beginning there.

Antioch Being the Mortal Wound for Catholicism

Please take note that the beginning at Antioch was very crucial. If you know God, you must bow your head and worship Him every time you read Acts 13 and 14 because here is a very important matter. I will always sincerely thank God for Acts 13. Acts 13 is the mortal wound for Roman Catholicism. Without Acts 13 we would have to return to Rome whether or not Rome is right. Jerusalem became a center because the Holy Spirit initiated a beginning there. If the Holy Spirit had not initiated a beginning at Antioch, we would have to say that God had only one center on the earth.

Brothers, you must see the great significance of this matter. If you do not have the work on your heart, you will not feel that Acts 13 regarding Antioch is a great matter. But if you have the work on your heart, you will see that this was a very great step. This was a strategic step by the Holy Spirit. This was very crucial. Until the end of chapter twelve, all that can be seen is the work out of Jerusalem. Even the work at Antioch was out of Jerusalem. From chapter eleven we can see that the work in Antioch was done by brothers who came out from Jerusalem. Because of this we might spontaneously recognize that God's work on the earth had Jerusalem as its one center. This center might have moved somewhere else, but there would still be only one center. You would have had to admit that Christianity has a "capital." Just as Roman Catholicism claims that the capital of Christianity is Rome, Jerusalem would have become the capital of Christianity, in the same way that Mecca has become the capital of Islam, and Chufu has become the capital of Confucianism. But thank God, the Holy Spirit initiated another beginning at Antioch. The Holy Spirit sent out another group of apostles from Antioch.

Paul and Barnabas Becoming Apostles

How could Paul be so bold as to bear the name of apostle? Barnabas was a good brother, a common brother in Jerusalem;

he was not an apostle. Originally, Paul was also not an apostle. At Antioch the Holy Spirit designated both of them, set them apart, led the church to lay hands on them, and sent them out. After being sent out for a few days, they were both called apostles in Luke's record. Acts 14:4 says, "But the multitude of the city was divided, and some were with the Jews and some with the apostles." Here the word "apostles" is plural. The Holy Spirit did not say, "I ordain you, I establish you, to be apostles." It was simply recorded that they were apostles.

Verse 5 says, "A hostile attempt was made by both the Gentiles and Jews with their rulers to treat the apostles outrageously and to stone them." The pronoun here in the original Greek is plural, referring to the apostles. The people wanted to treat the apostles outrageously and to stone them. Verse 6 says, "They became aware of it and fled to the cities of Lycaonia, Lystra and Derbe, and the surrounding region."

This beginning was initiated by God through His Spirit, not by Paul or Barnabas. If it had been a beginning initiated by Paul or Barnabas, we could deny it. But it was the Holy Spirit who initiated another beginning at Antioch, established another group of apostles, and sent two out to work. Therefore, it is clear that on the earth there was not only one but two regions of work. Hence, the thought that the earth has only one center of work is shattered. Christianity does not have a capital. Thank God! Where the Holy Spirit works, there the "capital" of Christianity is. No one can restrict the work of the Holy Spirit. The Lord is still the Head of the church; the Holy Spirit is still the Lord's representative. We are not here to be the representatives of the Holy Spirit. He often uses us, but there are also many times that He works without us. If Jerusalem wanted to be dictatorial about the Lord's work, it would not be able to. If Jerusalem wanted to monopolize the work of Christianity, it would not be able to. We have seen that God already established Jerusalem as a center, but God can also set up Antioch as a center. Therefore, God can set up Shanghai as a center, and God can also set up Foochow as a center. Here we can see that there is not one center only. If there were only one center, then the principle of Rome would be correct.

The Possibility of a Third Region Being Set Up

Brothers and sisters, this is most crucial. Acts 13 is the foundation of Christianity. Without Acts 13 we cannot say how many problems would have occurred. Without Acts 13 the concept of the pope would be entirely correct. The concept of Rome, the concept that there is a capital of Christianity, would be completely correct. But now we know that before God there was not only one center but two centers, not only one region but two regions. Therefore, when it pleases the Holy Spirit, He can establish a third region, a tenth region, a hundredth region, a thousandth region, or a ten-thousandth region on the earth. This is according to the intention of the Holy Spirit regarding His work on the earth; it is not according to man's intention.

Apostles Who Are Not Elders
Being Able to Continually Go Out

As I have said, it is interesting that these two apostles sent out from Antioch were not elders at Antioch. Therefore, if they wanted to work, they had to become travelers, continually going out from place to place. They also returned to Antioch, but they did not return very quickly. When Paul stayed in Ephesus, he stayed for three years. If they had been elders in Jerusalem when they went to Ephesus, they could have stayed for three weeks at the most before returning; they could have gone out from Jerusalem, but they would have had to return soon after. Because they were apostles, they could go out. But if they had been elders, they would have had to return.

Paul and Barnabas were apostles. Therefore, they went out. It could be a long time before their return because they were not elders at Antioch. This is very clear.

Peter and John were both apostles and elders in Jerusalem. For this reason, whenever they went out, they had to return quickly because the responsibility of Jerusalem was upon them. They had to go out because they were apostles. They could not help but return because they were elders. This is very significant. Let me tell you, this is a beautiful thing.

Because they were apostles, they continually went out. Because they were elders, they continually returned. They could not go too far because they had to bear the local burden in Jerusalem.

Paul and Barnabas were only apostles, not elders. Therefore, they could go out for a period of years without any problem. Wherever the Holy Spirit led them, they could go because they were only apostles and not elders.

NEEDING A STRONG MEETING

Why do we need to spend so much time to talk about this one matter? It is because this has much to do with our work. We must receive this principle. If we begin to bear responsibility in a region and establish local churches there, we need to learn to be apostles, on the one hand, and elders, on the other hand. This is because we need to have a strong meeting in this region. Many Bible expositors have often told us that Antioch was the strongest church at that time. Furthermore, many have told us that the church in Antioch was a model church. I remember that when I was young, there was a book called *The Model Church,* which spoke about Antioch.

If someone does not bear the responsibility in a local church, he must be an apostle exclusively, continually going out freely, and then returning. It does not matter if he takes a long time. However, some need to return soon after they go out, as Peter did when he went to Samaria and Caesarea. After a short time, he had to return because he was also an elder.

From now on, when brothers among us go out, you must remember that those who are apostles can go, but those who are elders need to return. I feel this way is very pure. It is definite with no difficulties.

THE GENERAL LOCAL CHURCH
AND THE LOCAL CHURCH AT THE CENTER OF THE WORK
DIFFERING SLIGHTLY IN THE MATTER
OF THE MESSAGE MEETING

The local church in this locality is still the same as the

local churches elsewhere. If there is a difference, the difference is that there are apostles living in the regional center. Perhaps at the same time these apostles are also elders. Once you have clearly seen this point, you can realize that there may be a slight difference between the general local church and the local church at the center of the work in the matter of the message meeting. Because the apostles are there, they may be willing to give a special supply, special messages, or special ministry of the word. There can be such a thing because the apostles are there. This is something that a general local church does not have. This is the difference between a local church at the center of the work and a general local church.

THE APOSTLES ALSO BEING ELDERS

I think we must recognize that when the co-workers met at Hankow, the light regarding Jerusalem was still not sufficient. Of course, there are still many other things that we have not seen. But today at least we can say that we see the light concerning Jerusalem which we did not see in Hankow. We can now add to it. We see that the church is local and that the work is regional. God chooses a locality to be the center of the work. The church in that locality is slightly different from the churches elsewhere because there are apostles who are also elders in that locality.

This is what we wanted to bring up concerning the arrangement of a local church at the center of the work.

CHAPTER NINE

THE RELATIONSHIP BETWEEN
THE LOCAL CHURCH, THE WORK,
AND THE APOSTLES

What is the relationship between the local church and the work? What is the relationship between the local church and the apostles? We want to pay special attention to these matters. Local churches such as those in Jerusalem and Antioch are special and exceptional because, on the one hand, they are local churches, and on the other hand, they are centers for the work. As local churches they are the same as other churches. As to the work they are also centers for the work. Therefore, we have to recognize that Jerusalem and Antioch are somewhat different from other local churches. However, regarding other local churches, what is their relationship with the work?

In *The Normal Christian Church Life* we made quite an effort to show the brothers and sisters that the local church is the highest authority on earth. The Lord has not established a federated church, a mother church, or a head church above the local church. There is no such concept in the Bible as a mother church or a head church. In the Bible only a local church is recognized as a unit. In addition, the local church is recognized in the Bible as the unique unit. There is no authority above her.

THE ELDERS BEING THE HIGHEST AUTHORITY
IN A LOCAL CHURCH

In a local church the highest authority is the elders. All the matters are handled by the elders. The apostles cannot directly interfere with a local church; they cannot deal with the affairs of a local church. For example, there was a person in Corinth who needed to be removed, and yet Paul could not remove him. This is a very crucial example. Do you see from this the relationship between the local church and the work, as well as the relationship between the local church and the apostles? In other words, what the apostles want to do must go through the elders; the things which the apostles want to do cannot be done directly. God has not asked a local church to receive the commands of the apostles directly. God only asks the brothers and sisters in a local church to receive the commands of the elders. If the spiritual condition of an elder is right, he should receive the commands of the apostles. On the spiritual side the elders should listen to the apostles.

The Elders Being Appointed by the Apostles

We need to pay special attention to the point that the apostles appoint the elders. The elders in all the localities are appointed by the apostles. Timothy and Titus were apostles; they were sent by Paul. These two, one in Ephesus and one in Crete, traveled in the surrounding areas and appointed elders in various localities. Therefore, the authority of the elders is not received from the church. You must make the churches in the various localities see that not one local overseer is elected locally. My father is my father not because I voted for him, but because I was born of him. The Lord said, "You did not choose Me, but I chose you." The elders are not chosen by the brothers in the church but are appointed by the apostles. A local church should not select elders; it has neither the authority nor the knowledge to do so. The local brothers are absolutely not allowed to select some to oversee them. There is no such thing! What God has shown us is that it was Paul, Timothy, and Titus who appointed elders. The elders are appointed by the workers from without.

The Church Listening to the Elders and the Elders Learning to Listen to the Apostles

Once a local church has had elders appointed, it should listen to the elders, not to Timothy and Titus. The elders are the overseers of the church. The highest authority in a local church is the elders; however, the authority of the elders is

THE CHURCH, THE WORK, AND THE APOSTLES   143

received from the apostles. The apostles give the authority to the elders, and the elders administrate the local church directly. Therefore, everyone who is an elder, an overseer, must learn to listen to the apostles. Because their being elders is due to the apostles, they cannot overthrow the authority of the apostles. It is all right for the church not to receive the commands of the apostles directly, but it is not all right for the church not to receive the commands of the elders directly. However, the elders need to learn to listen to the apostles. This is what God has arranged with respect to the local church.

The Apostles
Being the Ones to Remove the Elders

After the meeting in Hangkow, some brothers misunderstood. They thought that though the elders are appointed by the apostles, they did not have to listen to the apostles. This is impossible. When there were brothers who did not respect the elders and problems occurred, the letter of accusation by two or three was sent to Timothy. In other words, the authority for the appointment of the elders is with the apostles, and the authority for the removal of the elders is also with the apostles. A local church cannot expel an elder; rather, the apostles need to bear the responsibility of removing elders. This is the reason why the letter of accusation by two or three was sent to Timothy.

Why is there the need of two or three people? Because this is not a matter of personal opinion. Some people speak loosely, and this is not allowed. There is the need of a letter of accusation by two or three in order to oppose a brother. This makes it a sufficiently troublesome matter. At least two or three accusers are needed to accuse an elder. Why is a letter of accusation used instead of spoken words? Spoken words can easily become rumors; but since a letter of accusation is written down, it can become a formal accusation. Therefore, there must be a letter. In this way, one cannot speak loosely. Anyone who does things loosely must bear the responsibility for it.

THE APOSTLES BEARING
THE RESPONSIBILITY FOR THE WORK
AND THE ELDERS BEARING
THE RESPONSIBILITY FOR THE CHURCH

Here you can see that the apostles appoint the elders, and the apostles also remove the elders. However, the direct administration of a local church is not in the hands of the apostles; it is in the hands of the elders. The apostles bear particular responsibility for expanding the work, not for administrating business affairs. The administration and care of a local church are the responsibility of the elders, not the apostles. The apostles take care of carrying out the work of the church as a whole. The Bible makes a clear distinction between the workers, the local churches, and the elders concerning their limit of authority, the arrangement of their work, and their coordination. Therefore, we are here to try to find out the way to go on properly.

HOW THE CHURCH MAKES DECISIONS

A brother once asked how a matter should be decided in the work or in the church after it has been discussed. I think that every worker or every elder in a locality has the common feeling that a message meeting is rather easy but a business meeting is difficult. There is no problem when it comes to spiritual matters. The greatest problem is with the business meeting, because in that kind of meeting, it is very easy for everyone to have his own view; everyone's opinion is different. Many of the problems lie especially with the matter of decision making.

ACTS 15—THE PATTERN FOR A CHURCH CONFERENCE

Today I want to show you, as I have spoken in these past few months, that Acts 15 is the only place in the entire Bible which records a meeting in which the church discussed business affairs. While there have been many councils in the Catholic Church, there was only one such conference in Jerusalem. The entire church has had only one such conference. God specifically placed this unique conference in the Bible to be a pattern. Hence, you should never make the mistake of considering that chapter fifteen of Acts is not so good. Rather, you need to realize that chapter fifteen is the most precious chapter in the whole book of Acts. Without Acts 15, we simply would not know what to do when we tried to handle business affairs. It is very good that Acts 15 has been set before the church. The pattern given to us by this unique instance is the pattern accepted by the church for the past two thousand years. We acknowledge that this is the highest pattern.

Some Problems

In Acts 15 a problem arose. Many foolish brothers think that being free from problems is a sign that a church is spiritual. But please keep in mind that the sign of a church being spiritual is not that it is free from problems. Instead, the sign of a church being spiritual depends upon whether it has ways to solve problems and whether those ways are appropriate. If the church is spiritual, many things will happen to it. Once a church becomes spiritual, many problems will have to be considered. If a church is not spiritual, any way and any thing is all right. If a church is not spiritual, it is peaceful and without problems. The more one lies under the hand of the "strong man," the more peaceful his situation is. The more spiritual you are, the more problems you have to solve.

Jerusalem had a problem. Where did that problem come from? Many people who formerly were zealously serving Judaism went to different places. Some went to Antioch and told people that the believers in the church should also be circumcised according to the regulations of Moses. Under these circumstances both Paul and Barnabas had to go to Jerusalem, and other brothers in the church in Antioch also went up with them.

Brothers Being Allowed to Speak
in the Conference of the Apostles and Elders

I want you to pay special attention to the fact that when they went up to Jerusalem, they went up to see the apostles and elders. Acts 15:2 speaks of going up to "the apostles and

elders in Jerusalem." Verse 4 says, "And when they arrived
in Jerusalem, they were received by the church and the
apostles and the elders." The church, the apostles, and the
elders, all three, received them.

Some of the believers were former Pharisees. Their background was Pharisaic. They stood up to say, "It is necessary to
circumcise them and to charge them to keep the law of Moses"
(v. 5). I want the brothers and sisters to see how matters were
discussed in the conference recorded in the Bible. The conference in Jerusalem was a conference of the apostles and elders;
it was not a conference of the church. The responsibility was
on the apostles and the elders. Of course, such a thing was no
problem to the apostles and elders. But a few believers, who
formerly were Pharisees, rose up and said that they wanted
the Gentiles to be circumcised and to keep the law. I want
the brothers to pay attention to this matter that it was the
apostles and the elders who played the primary role in discussing matters in the church and that it was also the apostles
and elders who later made the decision in these matters. But
when the apostles and the elders made decisions, they had to
listen to the opposing brothers. The apostles and elders could
have very easily made a decision on this matter. They had no
problems; they were very clear before God. But a few believers,
formerly Pharisees, felt that believers should still be circumcised and keep the law. What did the church in Jerusalem do?
The apostles and elders of Jerusalem met and also allowed
these brothers to come and present their arguments. You
should give those who oppose and who have different opinions
the opportunity to speak by telling them, "Speak as much as
you wish." Never consider that this is not spiritual. God desires
that the responsible brothers, the brothers with authority,
would be those who can listen to others. The responsible
brothers, the brothers with authority, should have the ability
to sit and listen to all the opposing words. If a brother cannot
listen to the speaking of others, to the arguments of the
opposers, then he is not qualified to be a leader in the church.

Hence, you can see that "the apostles and the elders were
gathered together to see about this matter" (v. 6). The former
Pharisees still advocated the practice of circumcision and the

keeping of the law. The phrase "when much discussion had taken place" implies that much effort was made, many words were spoken, various arguments were presented, and different views were made known. Many brothers agreed that the believers should be circumcised, and many brothers disagreed. The apostles and elders allowed the brothers who had opinions and the brothers who wanted to speak to present their views. Although this meeting belonged to the apostles and elders, they allowed the brothers to speak and allowed anyone who wanted to come to attend. Those who wanted to speak were given the opportunity to express their opinions. This is the principle by which things are settled in the Bible. Never annul a person's speaking, and never refuse to listen to others. Even if their words are weak or irrelevant, you still need to let them speak and present their opinions. But they cannot make the decision. In this way, at least when the brothers whose spiritual condition is proper, that is, the responsible brothers, listen to those words, they will know how to make a decision. Many responsible brothers in the church lack this habit of listening to others. They may only listen to one person's words or to a few men's words, but they never listen to everyone's words. The church is neither autocratic like Thyatira, the Roman Catholic Church, nor is it democratic like Laodicea. The church is in the principle of Jerusalem. The principle of Jerusalem is all the brothers speaking, with the responsible brothers making the decision.

The Decision Made by the Apostles and the Elders and Endorsed by the Holy Spirit and the Church

It is quite strange to see how the matter was decided. After the brothers and sisters had all spoken, the apostles and elders had to make the decision. The first one who stood up was Peter. Peter stood up to state his personal opinion, relating to them what he had personally experienced, saying, "Men, brothers, you know that from the early days God chose from among you that through my mouth the Gentiles should hear the word of the gospel and believe. And God, the Knower of hearts, bore witness to them, giving them the Holy Spirit even as also to us; and He made no distinction between us and them, cleansing their hearts by faith. Therefore why are you now testing God by placing a yoke upon the neck of the disciples which neither our fathers nor we were able to bear?" (vv. 7-10).

Later, they invited Barnabas to speak because Barnabas had gone out from Jerusalem. They asked him to relate the actual situation of the matter. Then Paul spoke.

You can see that here Peter spoke, Barnabas spoke, Paul spoke, and finally James stood up. Verse 13 is the best part: "And when they finished speaking, James answered, saying, Men, brothers, listen to me." He was the brother who was foremost in the church in Jerusalem. The history of the church shows us that at that time he was acting somewhat like a chairman, although this may not be the right term for it. Among the many brothers in Jerusalem at that time, James was the one who stood in the forefront. Peter, Barnabas, and Paul had testified, and the three were one. These three brothers with spiritual weight shared the same feeling. Let us see what James said: "And when they finished speaking, James answered, saying, Men, brothers, listen to me. Simeon has related how God first visited the Gentiles....Therefore I judge [these were words of authority] that we do not harass those from the Gentiles who are turning to God, but that we write to them to abstain from the contaminations of idols and fornication and what is strangled and blood. For Moses from ancient generations has in every city those who proclaim him in the synagogues, he being read every Sabbath. It then seemed good to the apostles and the elders with the whole church..." (vv. 13-14, 19-22). The matter was thus decided. This was the first, as well as the last, conference of the church recorded in the Bible.

I want to show you that this is how matters are decided in the church; it is not as the worldly people practice. The people of the world decide matters according to the opinion of the majority. The church does not decide matters in the way of Thyatira either, where one or two persons at the top make a decision and that decision is final. Rather, all the brothers have the opportunity not only to speak but even to discuss. First, everyone who wants to speak is allowed to speak. To do it this way does not mean that their words are taken but that the church waits on the mind of God. Perhaps a very simple brother speaks forth God's mind. Therefore, everyone may speak and discuss, but do not let the discussion continue the whole time. After much discussion and after many words have been spoken, let the responsible brothers, those who have spiritual weight before God, the elders and the apostles, speak forth their opinions. At the end God expresses His mind through the ones with the highest authority. You can see that the responsible brothers all had the same opinion. After hearing so much, with the opinions of all the responsible brothers being the same, they made the decision. The other brothers then needed to learn to accept this opinion. Thus, it says, "It then seemed good to the apostles and the elders with the whole church" (v. 22). This is how the affairs are handled in the church.

The church does not take care of its affairs by casting ballots. The final decision in handling affairs in the church is left with those who have spiritual weight. All the arguments are to be listened to; all the arguments of the brothers need to be heard. This is the manner of handling church affairs. Therefore, we need to learn to let them speak, to listen to all their arguments. I wish that every worker could listen patiently. If several brothers have opinions, let them speak and discuss. Never consider this to be wrong; this is a proper way. But at the same time, ask God to give you proper judgment.

Eventually, the decision of the apostles was readily seen as God's decision. Therefore, the words in verse 28 are very wonderful: "For it seemed good to the Holy Spirit and to us." The anointing of the Holy Spirit was there. That decision was made by the Holy Spirit and "us." A decision was made by the Holy Spirit and "us" to ask the apostles and the elders to write a letter.

Therefore, I hope you brothers can see that the way the church handles its affairs should neither be autocratic nor democratic. Neither autocracy nor democracy is allowed. There should be neither the opinion of only one person nor the casting of ballots. When the church handles affairs, the final decision rests with those who have spiritual authority. However, everyone should be given the opportunity to speak. While they are speaking, you are observing and sensing how their spirit is. At the end you stand up and say, "Brothers, concerning this matter, we few brothers have decided in this way." In the church there is neither the majority listening to the minority nor the minority listening to the majority. In the church there are only the brothers and sisters expressing opinions and the spiritual men making the decisions. After a decision, the church carries it out in one accord. This way is different from worldly organizations and methods. I hope that all the brothers and sisters can see this.

TOUCHING THE SPIRIT OF THE BIBLE

The most crucial thing in studying the Bible is to touch the spirit of the Bible. The basic requirement in studying the Bible is that a person touch the spirit of the Bible. Try to touch the spirit of Acts 15. We have seen above that many brothers were there and that "much discussion" had taken place. Since the Bible says "much," it must have been quite much. Perhaps those who formerly were Pharisees and who later became Christians spoke many foolish words. The first person's spirit that I want you to touch is that of Peter.

Peter Not Being Affected by the Spirit of Debate

How did Peter speak when he stood up? He was not affected by those around him. As Peter stood to speak, he was like a newborn baby, free from any outside feeling and not at all affected by the spirit of debate. This should be the situation of the responsible brothers. If a responsible brother is affected inwardly, he is not qualified to bear the responsibility. Hence, the most important thing in reading the Bible is to touch the spirit of the Bible. When Peter stood up to speak at that time, he did not debate at all. Once you get involved with the debate, you are not qualified to be a leader, nor are you qualified to be one in authority. One in authority does not contend with people. Once you contend, you lose your position.

Peter stood up without any word of debate. This was

wonderful! Peter stood up to say, "Men, brothers, you know that from the early days God chose from among you that through my mouth the Gentiles should hear the word of the gospel and believe" (v. 7). Peter was saying, "This was what I told you some days ago. This is not something I say today. I have said it before." "And God, the Knower of hearts, bore witness to them, giving them the Holy Spirit even as also to us" (v. 8). Peter seemed to be saying, "I did not baptize them, nor did I lay hands on them. If I had baptized them, you would have said that this was something done by me. If I had laid my hands upon them, you would have said that it was I who gave them the Holy Spirit. I did not baptize them, nor did I lay hands upon them, nor did I pray for them; it was the Holy Spirit Himself who descended upon them. You cannot blame me for doing that." He further continued by saying, "And He made no distinction between us and them, cleansing their hearts by faith. Therefore why are you now testing God by placing a yoke upon the neck of the disciples which neither our fathers nor we were able to bear? But we believe that through the grace of the Lord Jesus we are saved in the same way also as they are" (vv. 9-11). His speaking was very clear, simple, and without any debate or spirit of debate.

Brothers, the Bible has its spirit, and you must touch that spirit in order to grasp that book. Peter simply presented his points without being affected or losing his dignity. He was like a person in authority, simply speaking forth these things. I hope you would see that in a conference of the church, if you slip into arguments, you will become like the others and be disqualified from making decisions.

Barnabas and Paul
Bringing In the Presence of God

Barnabas then stood up to speak, and Paul also stood up to speak. We need to pay special attention to the fact that when these two brothers stood up to testify, they had to be very serious before God. We must again try to touch their spirit. These two brothers definitely did not stand up to speak clamorously or lightly; they spoke with weight. We must understand the situation at that time. When Barnabas and Paul stood up to speak, their aim was to stop the contention, not to generate it. Contention is stopped by means of God's presence. In this kind of meeting, idle talk must be stopped. Idle talk is stopped not by our speaking but by bringing people before the Lord. If we are not this kind of person, such a conference will break down. It is useless to imitate. When Barnabas and Paul stood up to speak, everyone was silent. When these two brothers stood up to speak, they could bring others before God. The other brothers were their seniors, but due to these two brothers standing up to speak, everyone was brought before God, and God's presence was brought into the meeting. The noise of debate stopped, and everyone listened quietly to what God had done through their hands.

Paul had stood many times before crowds and before the Gentiles. There is no way to bring God's presence to such people that they may sense it, yet every servant of God is able to bring God's presence into the church of God. When His presence is brought into the church of God, everyone is silent. I hope that the brothers would see this basic principle. Never think that you can use words to deal with words, opinions to deal with opinions, reasonings to deal with reasonings, and contentions to deal with contentions. If you take that position, you will fail immediately.

Peter, who started first, stood up to speak, and his spirit was not at all affected by the debate of the brothers. He showed the brothers from the beginning what his situation actually was before God. While he stood there, he spoke as one who knew God's authority. As a result, he opened a way for Barnabas and Paul to speak. When these two spoke, they brought in God's presence and everyone became silent. When God's presence comes and the authority comes, all the opinions disappear. When God's authority is absent and God's presence is absent, any kind of conference in the church will not be carried out well. Man's opinions are full of confusion. Each one expresses his own view. But when God's authority comes in, everyone becomes silent.

Verse 12 says that they "became silent." At that moment only Barnabas and Paul spoke.

James Bringing In
the Feeling in God's Presence

After all were silent—I particularly like the words here—
"James answered" (v. 13). This was the final authority. He
was generally recognized as the leading one among the
brothers. He stood up and spoke in a simple way. You can
see that the meeting was in his hands. "Men, brothers, listen
to me. Simeon has related..." (vv. 13-14). After he repeated
the words of Peter, he quoted a verse from the Scriptures.
This is what God's Word says. Verse 19 then says, "Therefore
I judge." He gave a judgment. His opinion was, "Do not harass
those from the Gentiles who are turning to God." This was
not a word of debate or of contention; rather, he brought in
God's presence and God's authority; he brought in God's word
and the consideration and the feeling before God. It was in
this way that the conference of the church succeeded.

Not Merely Learning the Biblical Practice,
but Possessing the Spirit of the Bible

The brothers and sisters need to learn the things in the
Bible. Do not merely learn the method of the things; learn
the spirit of the things also. If we only have the method
without the spirit, the method is useless. We need to have
the method and at the same time we need to imitate the
spirit of the people in the Bible. There must be that spirit
and that presence. If we live in that reality, we will be able
to stop the speaking of the talkative ones in the meeting. If
we are loose and casual, if God's presence is not evident with
us, if God's authority upon us is not clear, if our attitudes,
words, and actions are all casual, this kind of meeting will
not have a good result. If the flesh cannot be restricted in
us, neither can the flesh be restricted in the meeting. If we
cannot bind our own flesh, neither can we bind the flesh of
the brothers. If we do not allow God's presence to be
manifested in us, submitting ourselves under God's authority,
neither can we cause all the brothers to submit themselves
under God's authority. It is a matter of our spiritual condition.
If our spiritual condition is proper, the result will be proper.

If our spiritual condition is not proper, the result also will not be proper. We may want to take Acts 15 as a method, but there is not one thing in the Bible that can be used as a method. The words in the Bible are definitely not a formula. If we work according to a formula, even if it is useful, the result is still void of spirit. It is not a matter of method, but a matter of spirit; it is not a matter of a formula, but a matter of spirit. It is not that when you go out you know how to deal with the situations you encounter; rather, it is that you live before God and thus are able to bring the entire meeting before God. If you do not live before God, you cannot bring the entire meeting before God. You may know the correct order of the procedures: Peter spoke first, Barnabas spoke second, Paul spoke third, James made the final decision, and the responsible brothers wrote the letter; however, the Bible does not give any ground to those who are not spiritual. You cannot be a person who is not spiritual and yet merely learn the methods in the Bible. You need to learn to capture the spirit; then you can go forward with all the things falling into place spontaneously.

Sometime later, when we come to the topic of reading the Bible, we will mention again that in studying the Bible the basic requirement is that we must connect with the spirit. Only when we connect with the spirit are we able to understand God's Word; otherwise, we cannot understand it.

CHAPTER TEN

THE COORDINATION AMONG THE WORKERS

RECOGNIZING AUTHORITY

Master Builders in God's Work

One thing we need to know is that even though there are many persons who are workers in God's work, some are manifested as master builders established by God. In 1 Corinthians 3:10 Paul said, "According to the grace of God given to me, as a wise master builder."

Those Who Lay the Foundation and Those Who Build upon It

In 1 Corinthians 3 some are building and some are laying the foundation. Therefore, Paul says, "As a wise master builder I have laid a foundation, and another builds upon it." Everyone is a builder; some lay a foundation, and some build upon it. Therefore, the workers should not work according to the way they want. It seems like some have been assigned to lay a foundation, and others have been assigned by God to build upon it. By this we see that some are master builders.

The meaning of the foundation is as follows: Those who lay a foundation have to find solid ground, to locate a site where they can lay the foundation. They go to find a place, they make arrangements related to the place, and they determine the position of the building site. There is no need for those who build upon the foundation to seek out a place or to determine where the best site for the building is. This is not the responsibility of those who build upon the foundation. Their responsibility is to build upon the foundation no matter where it is.

The Meaning of Not Building
upon Others' Foundation

When Paul said that he did not want to build upon others' foundation, he was specifically referring to the work of the brothers in the region of Jerusalem. Paul did not want to build upon their foundation, because he was a person established by God to be one who laid the foundation. But 1 Corinthians 3 shows us that others need to build upon Paul's foundation. In the future, at the Lord's judgment seat, they will be judged according to how they built upon it. Some use gold, silver, and precious stones to build, but some use wood, grass, and stubble to build. The judgment at the judgment seat will be a judgment of how one built upon the foundation.

Not Quoting the Word in a Light Way

Because many brothers and sisters have quoted in a careless way the words that I spoke from the Bible during the last few days, I feel bothered. There are words that you cannot quote in a careless way. If we have not attained to a certain state, we cannot apply certain words. We must advance to that state before we can say those words. They are not to be spoken by young people lightly. I have often heard young people say, "I do not want to build upon others' foundation." These words are quite out of place. In the Bible there are not that many people who have been raised up by God to lay a foundation.

This Word Being Spoken by Paul

No doubt, there were some brothers in Jerusalem who were raised up by God. Paul was also raised up by God. For Paul to say that he did not build upon others' foundation was right and was also to be expected because he was a master builder set up by God for the purpose of laying a foundation. If all of God's children wanted to lay a foundation rather than build upon the foundation, this would result in what is described in Hebrews 6, that is, continually laying a foundation without any building upon it. Paul said that he came to lay a foundation. He said, "I came and I have laid a foundation. I was sent by God." He said that he was an intelligent master builder, a wise master builder. Paul was not standing on an imaginary position. God actually established him. He was bold to make such a statement, and he was indeed a wise master builder who laid a foundation upon which others needed to build.

All of the brothers and sisters after Paul need to learn to build upon this foundation. In the future when you are judged, you will not be judged according to whether the foundation was right or wrong, but you will be judged according to how you built upon the foundation. When the judgment comes, it will be based upon whether you built upon the foundation with gold, silver, and precious stones or with wood, grass, and stubble. It will not be based upon whether the foundation was right, but on whether what was built upon it was right. Therefore, we should not say loosely that we do not build upon others' foundation. Paul could say this, but others cannot. We have seen that whoever lays a foundation is a wise master builder. The brothers after Paul should build upon the foundation laid by Paul. Building upon the foundation is their responsibility, while laying a foundation was Paul's responsibility. This is quite clear, and we need to learn this.

SOME TAKING THE LEAD AMONG THE APOSTLES

You need to keep in mind that Paul was an apostle and that Barnabas was also an apostle when he went out with Paul. In the Bible, just as I said a few days ago, there is no chief apostle. There is no position of a chief apostle. But in the Bible we can see clearly that some take the lead among the apostles.

Andronicus and Junia

Romans 16 implies this thought. That chapter clearly states that Andronicus and Junia were notable among the apostles. Some are especially notable among the apostles, and others are not.

Peter

Among the twelve apostles it was apparent that Peter was taking the lead. The twelve apostles did not stand up at Pentecost at the same time. Peter stood up first; then the eleven apostles stood up together with him. You need to pay attention to the order in the Word of God. A great multitude came to Jerusalem during Pentecost. When they heard the sound out of heaven, they were surprised. Wondering what it was, they all gathered at the place where the apostles were. The Bible recorded that Peter standing up together with the eleven, lifted up his voice to speak. Peter stood up, and the eleven apostles stood up with him. Peter was the one who lifted up his voice to speak. Among these twelve, there was spontaneously a leading one.

In the record of Acts 3, the Spirit of God placed Peter's name first when describing Peter and John going up together to the temple. Though the beggar saw both Peter and John, Peter's name always appears first. Both Peter and John together gazed at the beggar, but Peter spoke, not John. Later, Peter healed him, not John. At Solomon's porch Peter opened his mouth to preach, not John. Please remember that it was Peter who preached in chapter two, even though the eleven apostles were also standing there. The preaching in chapter three was also by Peter.

In chapter five it was Peter who dealt with the incident involving Ananias and Sapphira. Therefore, Peter took the lead all the way, even though the other apostles fellowshipped with God, communed before God, and labored together in oneness.

In chapter five, when the apostles were put in prison and then taken out to be judged, "Peter and the apostles answered and said, It is necessary to obey God rather than men" (v. 29). Again it was Peter who spoke. Even if they were all speaking, the Bible specifically says, "Peter and the apostles answered and said." I want you to read all these portions, and then you can see that the first section in Acts pays special attention to the matter of Peter being in the forefront.

Later, a great persecution occurred in Jerusalem, and the

disciples were all scattered abroad. They went about preaching the gospel, and some Samaritans received the Lord's word. When the church in Jerusalem heard this and sent out workers to them, it was again Peter and John who went together. Up to this point, it was still Peter who took the lead. Acts 10, concerning the events at the house of Cornelius, is a portion of the Word with which we are more familiar. Even though there were twelve apostles, only Peter was sought for. God's vision was also given to Peter. Later, we see that Peter took some brothers with him from Joppa, but the names of these brothers were not mentioned in the Bible.

Therefore, up to the point of Cornelius's house in Acts 10, God's way among the workers in Jerusalem was always that there was one who took the lead, and we can clearly see that this one was Peter.

Barnabas

Following this, the gospel was spreading in Jerusalem, Judea, and Samaria, and we see the conversion of Saul. Because the brothers in Jerusalem suffered persecution, some went to different places. Many people in these places believed in the word of the Lord. Therefore, the church in Jerusalem sent out another person, Barnabas, to go out and visit them. He went as far as Antioch. Barnabas was a good man, full of the Holy Spirit and of faith. When he arrived at Antioch, he helped the church in Antioch. After a period of time, Barnabas heard about Saul, and he went to Tarsus to seek for Saul and brought him to Antioch. Then Barnabas spent a whole year in Antioch. Barnabas did not have official duties in Jerusalem. That is why he could live outside of Jerusalem for a year. He did not have to return to Jerusalem like Peter or John, because he was not an elder in Jerusalem. We can say that, within this year, Saul received edification from Barnabas.

After a period of time, due to a great famine, the brothers in Judea became quite poor and suffered greatly. The brothers in Antioch sent money to the elders in Jerusalem through Barnabas and Saul. Because the money was for local use, it was sent to the elders instead of the apostles.

Later, several prophets and teachers were raised up in the church in Antioch. Barnabas was one of them, and Saul was also one of them. Then the Holy Spirit ordered that Barnabas and Saul be set apart to be apostles and sent out to work.

Up to this point, Barnabas was in the forefront. It was Barnabas who established the church in Antioch. The church in Antioch was not established by Saul. It was Barnabas who came down from Jerusalem to establish the church in Antioch. When the church in Antioch sent money to Jerusalem, they sent it through Barnabas and Saul. Saul was the one who followed. When the Holy Spirit came to send people out to work from among the prophets and teachers, the Scripture says, "The Holy Spirit said, Set apart for Me now Barnabas and Saul for the work to which I have called them" (Acts 13:2). Barnabas was still in the forefront.

God Being the God of Authority and the God of Order

Please remember that in God's work and in the church of God there can never be a situation in which there is no order. We need to see before God that even with two people, one is put ahead of the other. When ten people are together, there will be one in front and nine in the back. When twelve are together, one will be in front and eleven will be in the back. God is always the God of authority and the God of order. There is never a committee system of three or five men. There is no such thing in the Bible! There may be several elders, but God does not establish a committee. Although God does not set up a chairman, we need to listen to the one whom God establishes among the elders when carrying out the Lord's affairs. Today when we talk about the matter of the work, it is exactly the same. There were twelve apostles in Jerusalem, but God placed Peter in the forefront. The rest of the eleven had to wait in the back and listen to what he said. The James that we spoke of earlier was not the older brother of John. The older brother of John had already passed away. This James was in the forefront in the local church. We need to see this matter before God. Not only do we have Barnabas and Saul, but Barnabas was spontaneously ahead of Saul. In the work there are always those in the forefront. If two sisters have learned the lesson of recognizing authority, they will immediately realize that one of them needs to stand on the ground of obedience when they are together. The first thing in the coordination of the work is the coordination of the authority of God. Once we do not have the coordination of authority, all the other coordinations are empty.

Please note that God's word in the Bible is very fine and detailed. "God has placed some in the church: first apostles, second prophets, third teachers; then..." (1 Cor. 12:28). We must see that God is not a God of confusion but a God of order. God does not believe in disorder or confusion. God believes in order, and God is a God of authority. That is why He says "first." It does not mean that there is a system of organization or committees, in which everyone has the right to speak and vote. God does not recognize this at all. This is man's way. In His Word God says, "First...second...third... then...." This is the arrangement of God. Therefore, when the brothers come to work in the church or in any matter, they must see their own place. They must learn to line up. Today if three people are walking together, they should know spontaneously which brother is in front of them. If they have a question, they should ask that brother. This is the principle of the church here. It is very beautiful. When two or three brothers are together and something happens, some should immediately take the position of obedience and ask, "Since this matter must be decided, what do you say?" Even when two are together, we should know who stands before us. This is not a matter of ordination or assignment. If we have to assign, then things have been spoiled already. It is obvious that some stand in the forefront and some stand behind.

Being in the Forefront Is Having Authority

It is not God's intention that we listen to the authority that He has established because this person is perfect. Rather, God says that this person's authority is higher than ours; therefore, we need to listen to him. We do not listen to this person because he is more perfect than we are. We need to listen to him because he is in front of us. The basis for obedience is not that the one to whom you listen is perfect. The basis for obedience is whether or not the one to whom you listen is in front of you. If something goes wrong, he bears the responsibility. Let me illustrate. God says that wives must obey their husbands. The wife should not obey him on the basis of whether or not he is perfect. If husbands had to be perfect, all of the wives in the whole world would not need to obey their husbands, because no husband is perfect. The wife must obey her husband simply because he is the husband. Whether or not he is perfect is not the issue. The issue is whether or not he is the husband. If he is the husband, the wife needs to obey him—period. It is the same in the relationship and coordination among the co-workers in God's work. If two are put together, then they should spontaneously know their place. When something happens, we should always know when to stand aside and say, "Brother, you speak." We should wait for him to speak because he is in front of us. We are not obedient to man's selection, but we are obedient to God's authority. Once a brother stands in front of us, we should be obedient to him. It would be strange if there were no one to obey and if we could not even find someone to obey. If this is the case, we have absolutely not seen the arrangement of God's authority in the Bible.

This is the way when two brothers are together in the work: Spontaneously, Barnabas was in the forefront and Saul was behind. In the Holy Spirit's assignment, Barnabas was naturally put in front and Saul was behind. At the beginning of Acts 13, Barnabas was in the forefront the whole way when they went out. Verse 7 says, "Sergius Paulus...called Barnabas and Saul to him and sought to hear the word of God." Again, Barnabas is spoken of and then Saul.

In Acts 13:1, I would like for you to notice that Barnabas was the first one among many prophets and teachers and that Saul was the last. Do not think that Paul was advanced at the beginning. There is no such thing! When they went out, the last one was Saul. "Now there were in Antioch, in the local church, prophets and teachers: Barnabas and Simeon, who was called Niger, and Lucius the Cyrenian, and Manaen, the foster brother of Herod the tetrarch, and Saul." Barnabas was first, then Simeon, Lucius, Manaen, and lastly Saul. Among the five, the first was Barnabas and the last was Saul. Perhaps all of these others were ahead of Saul in the Lord at that time. When they went out, the Holy Spirit also recognized Barnabas to be in the forefront. "And as they were ministering to the Lord and fasting, the Holy Spirit said, Set apart for Me now Barnabas and Saul for the work to which I have called them" (v. 2). Again it is Barnabas and Saul.

Later, when they were on the way in verse 7, Sergius Paulus "called Barnabas and Saul to him and sought to hear the word of God." The Holy Spirit still recognized Barnabas as being in the forefront.

Paul

However, something very interesting occurred at this juncture. In verse 9 the Bible records that Paul was filled with the Spirit in the work for the first time. Paul's being filled with the Holy Spirit previously at his baptism was another matter. He repented, and he was saved and filled with the Holy Spirit. That was a different matter. But in verse 9, the Bible records for the first time that "Saul, who is also Paul, [was] filled with the Holy Spirit." Here God did something through Paul. Paul performed a miracle by causing a man to be blind.

Later, they came to Pamphylia and then to another place called Antioch, a place with a similar name, except that it was Pisidian Antioch. When they went into a synagogue on the Sabbath and sat down, the synagogue rulers asked them to speak. Then Paul stood up. In the previous instance Paul performed a miracle, and here he preached. This was the first time in Acts that someone preached other than Peter and Stephen. The Bible never records that Barnabas gave a long message. Up to this point, only Peter had given a few long messages in Acts. On the day of Pentecost, he gave one message in chapter two and a few messages in the following chapters until his message in the house of Cornelius. Other than the words of Peter and Stephen, the Bible does not record whatever was preached by others. The Holy Spirit, however, allowed Paul to step forward to speak a strong word; the Spirit used him to be a minister of the word.

From that point forward, the wording in the Bible begins to change. Acts 13:43 says, "And when the synagogue gathering had been dismissed, many of the Jews and the devout proselytes followed Paul and Barnabas." Do you see it? Paul is listed first.

Verse 46 says, "And Paul and Barnabas spoke boldly," and verse 50 says, "But the Jews...raised up a persecution against Paul and Barnabas and cast them out from their borders."

But this does not mean that this matter was settled. When we come to chapter fourteen, Barnabas was mentioned first one more time. This occurred after they returned to Lystra. From chapter thirteen Paul was clearly in the forefront. Even in chapter fourteen Paul was in the forefront. It was Paul who preached and healed the lame man. Then verse 12 says, "And they called Barnabas, Zeus, and Paul, Hermes, since he was the one who took the lead in the discourse." Zeus and Hermes were the names of the gods of Lystra. The heathen saw that Paul was the leading speaker. Therefore, when they addressed him with a name of their god, they used a name with a higher status because he was the one speaking and taking the lead. Although verse 14 says, "Barnabas and Paul," with Barnabas being spoken of first, this is an exception. There is a reason for this exception: When the priest of Zeus (whose temple was outside the city) heard that Zeus had come down from heaven, descending upon a person, he came quickly, bringing bulls and garlands to the gates, and he wanted to sacrifice with the crowds to the apostles. They thought that Barnabas was Zeus; therefore, they put Barnabas in the forefront. The priest of Hermes did not come, but the priest of Zeus came to sacrifice to his own god. This is why verse 14 says, "But when the apostles, Barnabas and Paul, heard this, they tore their garments." It was natural for Barnabas to take the lead here, because the people thought Barnabas was Zeus. Therefore, Barnabas jumped into their midst before Paul.

Following this, we can see that the crowds originally were sacrificing to both apostles, but the apostles refused to accept such a thing. As a result, "Jews from Antioch and Iconium came there; and having persuaded the crowds, they stoned Paul and dragged him outside the city, supposing that he was dead." Formerly, they wanted to sacrifice to him, but now they tried to stone him to death. "But as the disciples surrounded him, he rose up and entered into the city. And on the next day he went out with Barnabas to Derbe." Paul was the center of this incident. From this point onward until chapter fifteen, Barnabas's name was placed ahead of Paul's only one more time. That incidence also had its own reason. Besides these two places, Paul always took the lead.

In chapter fifteen they returned to Antioch. What did they do when the trouble arose in Antioch? "No little dissension and discussion with them came about through Paul and Barnabas" (v. 2a). Later, when the brothers sent people to Jerusalem, "the brothers directed Paul and Barnabas and certain others among them to go up to the apostles and elders in Jerusalem concerning this question" (v. 2b).

Barnabas spoke first in the meeting and then Paul because Barnabas was one who had come out of Jerusalem. Therefore, Barnabas naturally spoke first in the meeting, and then Paul gave an answer. The weighty persons always speak later. Hence, those who speak later have a more respectable position. The last one who spoke was James.

The Bible says, "It then seemed good to the apostles and the elders with the whole church to choose men from among them to send to Antioch together with Paul and Barnabas" (v. 22). Paul was standing in the forefront, but when they wrote the letter, it was written by "Barnabas and Paul" (v. 25). Barnabas was in front. They could not have said that they sent Paul and Barnabas, because Barnabas was from Jerusalem. This is the reason.

After the problem in Acts 15 was resolved, it was still Paul and Barnabas, who "stayed in Antioch, teaching and

announcing the word of the Lord as the gospel with many
others also" (v. 35).

No Coordination without Obedience

We have spent only a little time to see that the matter
of who should be the leader and who should obey in the
work is spontaneously arranged before God. When Christians are together there should be fellowship as well as
obedience among them. We hope that brothers and sisters
can eventually learn that when two are together there will
always be one who obeys. When three people are together,
there will always be two who obey. This is the basic
coordination in the work. Without obedience there is no
coordination. When two or three brothers or eight or ten
brothers live together, we should never allow a confused
situation to exist in which they do not know whom they
should listen to. Such a confused situation would prove that
we have received very little instruction before God. Whenever
God's children live together, they will spontaneously and
immediately know whom they should listen to if they have
been instructed before God. When brothers live together or
when brothers fellowship together, spontaneously there is
one who is in the forefront among them. Whenever something
happens, learn to obey. Once we have learned this matter,
there is no need for man to tell us or teach us. We will
automatically stay in our position and ask, "Brother, what
do you think I should do?" After he speaks, the matter will
be settled and it will be arranged that way. We need to keep
our place, knowing what our position is and knowing that
this is what God wants us to do.

The first thing in God's work and in the coordination
among workers is to ask God to open our eyes that we may
know the authority among us. When we are together with
brothers, we should know which brother is ahead of us. We
need to humble ourselves to see that as soon as a word is
spoken, a matter is decided, or an opinion is expressed, we
need to obey. We are persons who obey. We are not here to
elect or nominate, but to stand spontaneously in our place.
Recognizing authority is the first principle of coordination. If

we do not recognize this fact, we will find that it is impossible to coordinate.

FELLOWSHIP BEING NEEDED

In coordination, the first matter is authority, and the second matter is fellowship.

Co-workers Being Those to Whom We Can Open Up Our Heart

A basic need among co-workers is that they be ones to whom we can open up our heart and with whom we can have fellowship. Coordination opposes individualism. Coordination is for the service of the Body. It is we who serve, but we serve according to the principle of the Body. Therefore, we need the mutual fellowship, having our hearts open to one another and helping one another. If a member rejoices, the entire Body rejoices. If a member suffers, the whole Body suffers. If a member is sorrowful, the whole Body is sorrowful. This is called coordination.

Two Persons Being as One Man

Several people living together is not necessarily coordination. Suppose a brother has a very thick, heavy, solid outer shell; whether he lives alone or with ten people, he remains an individual. This is not coordination, and he is not in coordination. Many people, whether they are alone or with ten people, pray, seek God, speak to God, and seek the will of God as individuals. How can we say that this is coordination? This is not coordination. Putting two people together as co-workers does not mean putting two individuals together. Do we see this? We must not have the misconception that this is coordination. Formerly, we worked by ourselves; now two are working together. If one person is working alone, he is working individualistically. If two persons are working together as two individuals, there is still no coordination. It is useless if one person is an individual or if two persons remain as individuals! Formerly, one person was working, but now two persons need to work together as one. When two or three get together, what should they do? They need to be in

one accord! This means that before God we are able to open
up to our brothers.

Needing to Disclose Our Affairs
to the Co-workers

Many brothers cannot pray with other brothers at all. No
one knows their affairs. They cannot open up to other
brothers. Many people can bear their difficulties alone. They
will not consult with other brothers. They may have many
difficulties, but when they encounter problems, they still hold
on to their individualism, thinking that they can handle their
own problems and solve them before God by themselves.
Please remember, we may live among brothers, but our spirit
may not be with the brothers. Our body may be among the
brothers, but we may not live like a member of the Body.

In order to coordinate we need to recognize authority, and
we absolutely need to know what fellowship is. To fellowship,
one should be able to open up to others. Such a one has
several co-workers by his side; they are the ones to whom he
opens his affairs. He can say to them, "Brothers and sisters,
I cannot get through in this matter. How should I take care
of it?" or "Brothers and sisters, I cannot get through in this
matter. Can you pray together with me?" Please remember,
people who cannot bear others' burdens cannot coordinate
with others. People who cannot open up their heart to others,
also cannot coordinate with others.

Needing to Bear Others' Burdens

Some people are full of their own burdens. There is
absolutely no way for them to bear anyone else's burden
because they only think about themselves day and night.
Whenever someone asks them to pray for him, they do not
pray. Whenever someone asks them to pay attention to a
certain matter, they do not take care of it; rather, they leave
that matter uncared for and unattended. If you ask them
how this matter should be handled, they have no heart to
pay any attention to it. There is no coordination with them
whatsoever. They still strongly hold on to their individualism.
Although they are members of the Body, they still act

independently. For example, if I cut off my finger and leave it in Nanking, it would be useless. Likewise, if I sever my leg so that it loses its oneness and fellowship with the body, it would be useless. The basic principle of the Body is fellowship. Therefore, the basic principle of the work is also fellowship.

We are used to accommodating ourselves, bearing our own responsibilities, and not paying attention to others' affairs. Today we need to learn to bear the burden of others and to bear the burden with others. We may feel that this is very difficult; we may feel that it is hard to obey others, and we may even feel that it is hard to fellowship with others.

Needing to Seek For Fellowship

I do not mean that some among us should not be responsible before God for our own affairs and that we should just cast these affairs upon other brothers. The word I have spoken is not to those who are lazy before God. It does not mean that we need not be desperate before God and that we need not seek and ask before God. It means that we are still responsible toward God, that we still draw near to the Lord, and that we still seek after Him. We should not cast our responsibility on others without bearing any of it ourselves. It means that when we bear our responsibility, we always seek fellowship with other brothers and sisters. When I see that there are important things that are very much related to my future, I need to say, "Brother, would you have some fellowship with me, consider with me, and seek together with me how I should handle this matter? Would you wait on the Lord together with me?" We should take up our own burden and also coordinate and fellowship with other brothers and sisters. We need fellowship and coordination not only in our daily living but also in the work.

We need to learn to be an open person. Many brothers and sisters can open up only after others open up. It is not easy to ask them to be an open person. Many people will open up only when others open up to them. It is good to have someone open up to you first, but you should also open up. You need to learn to be an open person.

Brothers and sisters, I can tell you this, that one day when you are really clear about the principle of fellowship, you will be amazed at how some Christians whom you consider not so capable can render you such great help. Those members whom you consider not very useful can strengthen your hand. This is something that you would never have thought of, something completely outside of your expectation.

Bringing In the Power
by Seeking the Lord with One Accord

For instance, if three, five, or eight brothers in the work are going to Tsingtao and all of them are still individuals, there is no co-working and there is no coordination. In the case of the brothers who are going to Wenchow, if each one is still individualistic and his spirit is not open to the others, it will be useless even though they may live together. It will be useful only when the twenty persons are as one. If twenty remain as twenty, that is useless because there is no coordination. When they get to Wenchow, if everyone is an open person and everyone seeks the Lord together with one accord, the power will come. If two or three seek with one accord in prayer, God will hear them. If each one prays his own prayer, this is not being in one accord. They may call themselves co-workers and live together, but each one is still wrapped tightly in himself and doing his own thing. If this is so, where is the Body on the earth? Where are the members on the earth? That is a paralyzed person with no living members!

Needing to Cast Off Individualism

Brothers, do you see? We need to cast off many things before we go back. Even our individualism has to be left here. We need to learn to be an open person. Toward our brothers, our spirit needs to be open, our thinking needs to be open, and many times even our mouth needs to be open. Many times because our mouth is shut, our spirit is also shut. There are people who have never asked for help in their entire life. While we are here on the mountain, I hope that those among us will ask for help at least once. I hope there will be those among us who can say to the brothers or sisters, "I have had trouble with this one matter for many years. Please help me overcome it." If this is the first time in our life that we ask for help, let it be here.

Oh, we do not know what proud persons we are! Many people simply do not realize how proud they are. Many people also do not realize how tightly they are wrapped in themselves. Many say that they are broken before God; however, if we turn them around and put them before other people, they are not broken in the least. Actually, if a person is broken before God, he is broken wherever he is. If a person has been broken before God, he is really broken. Asking for help is called fellowship, and we need to reach out to seek fellowship.

One should not cast off responsibility onto others. For such a person to petition and pray is useless. Those who are responsible and who seek after the Lord have learned to be broken before God and actively seek out the help of the members of the Body. Thus, when they go to another place, they will pray with others and will discuss and consider things together with others before God. Otherwise, what does it mean to be a co-worker? Actually, there would be no co-worker.

I am afraid that there are some brothers who cannot bear responsibility with anyone even after working for ten or twenty years. For ten or twenty years perhaps they have not had any co-workers or learned to bear responsibility with other people before God. Maybe they are proud to such an extent that they bear all the responsibility alone. Perhaps they do not care for the things of others; they do not have a heart for the things of others. Has there been one time when some brother shared a certain matter with you, and you brought this matter to God in prayer? Have you truly been burdened for one and fasted concerning his situation? Have you truly wanted to know God's will so that you could tell him, "This is how I feel"? Brothers, if we do not learn how to bear the burdens of others, and if we do not seek out the help from others regarding our own burdens, we do not know what the Body is, nor can we have coordination in the work.

I hope that you would seek the Lord and pray together

with some brothers and sisters when you go out to work in a region today. It is the best sign when you can pray together with others and when you hide nothing in your prayer. Of course, the problems of a personal nature that we deal with before God are another matter. However, in the work there are many things that we can pray together about and open to one another. We can bear each other's burdens. Sometimes you bear my burden, and sometimes I bear your burden. If we go out in this way, we can be at peace and thank the Lord that there is coordination.

If we stay in our former condition, we will still be tightly wrapped up in ourselves, and our outer shell will not broken. My affairs will still be my affairs, and I will not let you touch them. My work will still be my work, and I will not let you interfere. When problems come, you may go desperately to the Lord alone; this is right and necessary. However, have you never once sought out the help and supply of the co-workers? If only you go to God alone, you do not know the coordination of the Body, and it will be impossible for anyone to entrust any burden to you. You will always be busy bearing your own burden, and you will not be able to bear the burden of anyone else.

Whether or not the co-workers can pray together is the greatest test. The greatest test is whether or not the co-workers can discuss things before God in one accord: "I have this problem, and you have that problem; let us put all these before God together." I hope that from now on none of us will bear any burdens individually. Yes, we do need to bear burdens, but we cannot bear them in an individual way without seeking out fellowship. By all means, we need to learn to seek out fellowship.

The Head Giving the Authority, and the Members Having the Fellowship

The usefulness of the Body is in the fellowship. The first principle of the Body is authority, and the second principle is fellowship. The supply from the coordination depends on the supply from the authority and also the supply from the fellowship. What comes from the Head is authority, and what comes from the members is fellowship. The Head provides the authority so that we can have order in the Body and order in the church. However, there is also the mutual fellowship among the members. These are the basic principles. Fellowship is very important.

There are many brothers and sisters in our midst. I want to charge you again to test yourselves thoroughly concerning this matter: "O Lord, am I a person who closes up his heart and never asks for help?" Please remember that we cannot find such an aloof Christian in the entire Bible. Being aloof is not the way of a believer. Never think that you should take care of everything by yourself and not care about the matters of other brothers and sisters. You cannot be a Christian on the earth in this way. You need to learn from the beginning how to coordinate with the brothers in the work. This is the way to have spiritual usefulness. Otherwise, when twenty brothers go to Wenchow, they will still be twenty individuals, twenty units there, and when twenty brothers go to Tsingtao, there will still be twenty units there. If this is the case, their going will be useless. On the one hand, we need to learn to submit to authority, and on the other hand, we need to have fellowship to the extent that we can say, "Thank the Lord! Praise the Lord! We bear the burdens in one accord. We have fellowship, and we have the authority. When there are problems, we take care of them step by step and level by level in an orderly way."

Both authority and fellowship are needed. Neither can be lacking. If we go out to work and experience failure, we should realize that if there is no problem concerning authority, then there must be one concerning fellowship. The work is a matter of authority and fellowship.

AUTHORITY AND FELLOWSHIP IN THE BIBLE

In the New Testament there are many arrangements and much fellowship in God's work. Especially with Paul we can learn that there are many arrangements, and we can find a basic principle—in these arrangements there is authority and also fellowship. Therefore, if we spend some time to look into the record in the Bible, we can repeatedly see that there are many arrangements in which the young brothers should listen to instructions in the work. These arrangements denote authority and also fellowship. When a brother has received knowledge and light, he not only uses authority to send some brothers to carry things out, but he also fellowships knowledge and light with them. Brothers, have you seen this? The arrangements in the Bible do not only denote authority. If they did, Paul would have simply told his young co-workers to do something and they would have done it. In these arrangements Paul had light and knowledge before God, and he imparted them to his young co-workers. Therefore, on the one hand, we need to see that this is a matter of authority, and on the other hand, we need to see that it is a matter of fellowship, because Paul shared his knowledge with his young co-workers.

Sending Tychicus and Onesimus

Colossians 4:7-8 says, "All the things concerning me, Tychicus, the beloved brother and faithful minister and fellow slave in the Lord, will make known to you, whom I have sent to you for this very thing." Do you see? Tychicus was sent to Colossae by Paul. Verse 9 continues, "With Onesimus, the faithful and beloved brother." Here you see that Paul sent Tychicus and Onesimus to Colossae together.

In God's work the master builders have authority to send people. It is recorded in the Epistles that Tychicus was a very good brother. The book of Philemon tells us that Onesimus was a beloved brother. But both of them were sent by Paul.

Sending Timothy and Epaphroditus

Let us continue with Philippians 2:19: "But I hope in the Lord Jesus to send Timothy to you shortly, that I also may be encouraged by knowing the things concerning you." Verse 25 says, "But I considered it necessary to send to you Epaphroditus."

Here the sending of two other brothers is spoken of; one was Timothy and the other, Epaphroditus. Timothy was like a son to Paul, as was Onesimus, whom we mentioned earlier.

These two were young brothers, and Paul sent them out. Epaphroditus was a co-worker of Paul and was raised up after Paul was; therefore, Paul sent him. Thus, the Bible clearly shows us that in the coordination of the work, the leading workers are those who send people out. The young workers need to take orders. Only when the older ones have the assurance before God, can they send people out. Paul said, "I hope in the Lord Jesus to send Timothy to you shortly." He was very clear before the Lord that he should send Timothy; he was sending Timothy according to his hope in the Lord Jesus. I hope that you will learn something from this.

Tychicus Also Going to Ephesus

Ephesians 6:21 says, "But that you also may know the things concerning me, how I am doing, Tychicus, the beloved brother and faithful minister in the Lord, will make all things known to you." Tychicus was sent to Colossae earlier; now he was being sent to Ephesus. Verse 22 says, "Him I have sent to you for this very thing." Tychicus was also sent by Paul to Ephesus.

Entreating Titus and Sending Another Brother to Go with Him

At another time Paul entreated Titus to go to Corinth. Second Corinthians 12:18 says, "I entreated Titus and sent with him the brother." The word used here is quite interesting. This time he did not send Titus but entreated him to go. Paul often did not like to send people. This is what you can see in the book of Titus. Paul was a person with much authority as far as Titus was concerned. Titus was a young person and was sent out by Paul; Paul had much authority over him. But here Paul only entreated him. Sometimes there was only the entreating, not the sending. There are two brothers in this verse; Paul did not mention the name of the other brother whom he sent. Therefore, some were sent. Some were sent because of the assurance that Paul had before God. Some were left in a place like Titus. Paul entreated him to go. Titus went because he obeyed. He received the entreaty;

therefore, he went. This was different from Apollos in 1 Corinthians 16.

Urging Apollos, His Not Wanting to Go, but His Going in the Future

First Corinthians 16:12 says, "And concerning our brother Apollos, I urged him many times to come to you with the brothers; yet it was not at all his desire to come now, but he will come when he has opportunity." Do you see the beauty here? It is very beautiful! Paul entreated Titus, and Titus obeyed and went. Titus was a young man, so he obeyed the entreaty. Apollos was not a young man; he was about the same age as Paul. In other words, he and Paul were of the same generation. Cephas, though, was ahead of Paul. In the church in Corinth some said, "I am of Cephas"; some said, "I am of Paul"; and some said, "I am of Apollos." Apollos's standing in the church in Corinth was that he belonged to the same generation as Paul. For this reason he was entreated, not sent. Paul did not send Apollos. Paul could not send Apollos; he could only entreat him. Furthermore, Paul entreated him not only once, but again and again. The good point here is that Apollos did not go. Paul entreated him and said, "You go with the brothers." He urged him once, twice, and three times. Apollos was willing to go, but he said that he definitely could not go at that time. Apollos was quite serious that he definitely did not want to go at that time. But Paul added a word: He was quite certain that Apollos would go. This is very beautiful! The older ones should be entreated; if they do not listen, do not worry. They will go because this is their way before God.

Therefore, the entreating of Apollos in 1 Corinthians 16 and that of Titus in 2 Corinthians 12 are different. Paul could have ordered Titus, but he did not; rather, he entreated him. But Titus took Paul's entreaty as a command. Paul could entreat Apollos, even twice or three times, but Apollos did not go. However, Paul was certain that he would go. Thus, the arrangement of the work is such that there is the authority and the fellowship. This is very precious.

Controlling Timothy's Movements
and the Fellowship of Revelation

First Corinthians 16:10 says, "Now if Timothy comes...."
Verse 11 says, "But send him forward in peace that he may
come to me." In other words, give Timothy a message that
when he comes to you, you need to send him forward, and
that he needs to come to me. "For I am awaiting him with
the brothers." Paul was expecting that Timothy would come
with the brothers. Have you seen this? Paul was controlling
their movements in the work. He was clearly asking Timothy
to come to him. Therefore, toward younger brothers, the words
in the Bible are quite clear. We need to learn before God that
the authority established by God can control the movements
of the young brothers. However, among the older ones, there
is only entreaty, not commandment.

Let us look further at the Epistles to Timothy.

First Timothy 1:18 says, "This charge I commit to you,
my child Timothy, according to the prophecies previously
made concerning you, that by them you might war the good
warfare." This shows us clearly that in the case of Timothy,
Paul gave orders. This charge I commit to you, that you might
war the good warfare. To Timothy, Paul gave orders directly.

First Timothy 3:14-15 says, "These things I write to you,
hoping to come to you shortly. But if I delay, I write that you
may know how one ought to conduct himself in the house of
God, which is the church of the living God, the pillar and
base of the truth."

In chapter two Paul spoke of males and females. In chapter
three he spoke of elders and deacons. What was the reason
that he especially wrote of these matters to Timothy? He
said, "I am hoping to come to you, but I am afraid I might
be delayed. In case I am delayed, you would not know what
to do in the church; therefore, I am writing to you first. In
such a case, I am writing to you so that you may know how
one ought to conduct himself in the house of God." In other
words, Paul did not leave ground for Timothy to find a way
himself. Paul did not allow Timothy to do things according
to his own way. Have you seen this? Paul wrote to him: "When

I am present, you can ask me in person; when I am not
present, you can read my epistle. When I come, you can ask
me; but before I come, you can read my epistle."

Let me say again, there is the principle of authority, and
there is also the principle of fellowship. Because Paul was
an elderly brother, he had authority. Writing a letter to a
younger brother is fellowship. Because Paul knew before God
and Timothy did not know, Paul fellowshipped what he knew
with Timothy. When Timothy obeyed, he received the fellowship. Please remember that obeying does not mean losing
your position in the work. Obeying allows you to obtain what
the older brothers have obtained; obeying causes you to
gain the revelation that they have gained in the work.
According to your way, you may be wrong; according to their
way, you will not be wrong. Therefore, you should receive
guidance from them.

This kind of word is very common in the Epistles to
Timothy. We do not have time to study them in detail; we
will read only the portions concerning the outward way of
the work.

Second Timothy 4:9 says, "Be diligent to come to me
quickly." What we see here is neither discussion nor hope,
because we know that Paul was martyred not long after he
wrote 2 Timothy. This is Paul's last Epistle. Therefore, he
says, "Be diligent to come to me quickly."

Verse 10 says, "For Demas has abandoned me, having
loved the present age, and has gone to Thessalonica." Here
there was a rebellious one who went out.

What about the other two? "Crescens to Galatia; Titus to
Dalmatia." Perhaps both of these were sent to those places.

Verse 11 says, "Luke alone is with me." He only had Luke
there with him.

Needing to Bring Mark

Verse 11 continues, "Take Mark and bring him with you."
This is the Mark about whom Paul and Barnabas contended.
Remember that in Acts Barnabas wanted to take Mark with
them, but Paul disagreed because Mark went away when the
work was at a crucial time. In the beginning they went

together; but when the work was intense, Mark left, Mark got sick, and Mark was not able to work. Therefore, Paul did not agree to take Mark with them. At that time Barnabas wanted to take Mark with them, perhaps because Mark was his relative. Therefore, the two had a sharp contention, and they went their separate ways. The amazing thing is that later Barnabas did not have the opportunity to work with Paul, but Mark had such an opportunity. Remember that Mark later had learned many lessons from Peter. The Gospel of Mark was dictated by Peter and written down by Mark. Shortly before Paul's death, Paul said, "Take Mark and bring him with you." For what reason? "For he is useful to me for the ministry." Mark was profitable to Paul for the ministry.

Verse 12 says, "But Tychicus I have sent to Ephesus." This shows us that this was the arrangement of the work. Paul asked Timothy to come, he asked Timothy to bring Mark with him, and he also sent Tychicus to Ephesus.

Verse 20 says, "Erastus remained in Corinth." Do you see? Paul was the one who knew the condition of the work the best.

Leaving Trophimus at Miletus

"Erastus remained in Corinth, and Trophimus I left at Miletus sick." Trophimus is one of the famous sick persons in the New Testament. Epaphroditus was one, and Trophimus was another.

"Trophimus I left at Miletus sick." Many times sick persons need to obey; they cannot say that they want to move around. If they are sick, they must stop for a little while. Paul said that he left Trophimus at Miletus. It was better for him to be left at Miletus and not be occupied with so many things.

Concerning Timothy, Paul said "Be diligent to come before winter." Paul gave him a definite time limit. Do not decide for yourself when to come. Be diligent to come before winter.

Brothers, we should see that this way is very clear. A brother like Paul, who walked before God, should be obeyed by Mark, Timothy, and Trophimus. If so, spontaneously, we will see that there is fellowship in the church, and spontaneously we will also be able to understand what authority is.

Titus Being Left in Crete
and Being Diligent to Go to Nicopolis

Concerning Titus we do not need to say much. A few verses from the first and the last chapters of Titus are sufficient.

Titus 1:5 says, "For this cause I left you in Crete, that you might set in order the things which I have begun that remain and appoint elders in every city, as I directed you." Are we clear? Titus was a young brother. In 2 Corinthians Paul indicated that he had entreated him to go to Corinth. They went to Crete together. Then Paul left Titus in Crete to complete the unfinished business. Paul told him how to set in order the things that were lacking, as he charged him. Here we can see authority and also fellowship.

Titus 3:12 says, "When I send Artemas to you or Tychicus, be diligent to come to me at Nicopolis, for I have decided to spend the winter there." Do you see? This is the way of the work. Paul said, "I want to send one of two brothers to you, maybe Artemas or Tychicus. It has not been fully decided; in any case, one will come to you. When he gets there, you need to come to me quickly in Nicopolis."

Here we see how an elderly brother arranged many things and how a young brother listened to his word.

Charging Timothy to Keep the Commandment

Finally, we should say more concerning what Paul said to Timothy.

First Timothy 6:13-14 says, "I charge you before God, who preserves all things in life, and Christ Jesus, who testified the good confession before Pontius Pilate, to keep the commandment spotless." You see how weighty a matter this is— "I charge you before God, who preserves all things in life, and Christ Jesus, who testified the good confession before Pontius Pilate, to keep the commandment spotless."

Verse 20 says, "O Timothy, guard the deposit." The commandment that I gave you, you need to guard.

Please remember that the young brothers need to learn what has been entrusted to the older brothers and learn to obey them. Then they will be able to walk the way ahead of them in a good way.

Paul Also Needing Fellowship

I hope that we can see how the work was carried out in the New Testament. The work in the New Testament is one that has arrangements, authority, and fellowship. I believe you still remember what I told you some days ago. Even though Timothy was a young brother, do you remember what was recorded in the book of Acts concerning what Paul did when Timothy came to him? "When both Silas and Timothy came down from Macedonia, Paul was constrained by the word, solemnly testifying to the Jews that Jesus was the Christ" (18:5). I feel that in the Bible this verse is the best. Paul was one who knew the Lord and was used much by Him. Yet because Silas and Timothy came down from Macedonia, he was constrained by the word. With Paul, fellowship was also necessary. When Timothy and Silas came, it was a great encouragement to him. This is what you can see from Acts 18.

Acts 17:14 says, "And immediately the brothers then sent Paul off, to go as far as the sea." Here Paul listened to the brothers' word. "And Silas and Timothy remained there." "There" refers to Berea, which is the name of a city in Macedonia. Macedonia is the name of a region, and Berea is the name of a city. Verse 15 says, "And those who conducted Paul brought him as far as Athens; and receiving a command for Silas and Timothy to come to him as quickly as possible, they went off." Paul commanded Silas and Timothy to come to him as quickly as possible. But after Paul went to Corinth, and after Silas and Timothy came to Corinth from Macedonia, Acts 18:5 says that Paul was constrained by the word. You see how good that situation was!

I hope that you brothers can see this principle in the work. Today we are like children learning to walk—step by step, slowly walking before God. I hope that all the children of God would know how to have the mutual coordination in the work; then we will be able to do the work in a good way.

CHAPTER ELEVEN

WHO OUR CO-WORKERS ARE
AND WHO THE APOSTLES ARE

Today we have two questions which we want to resolve:
Who are our co-workers, and who are the apostles?

A GREAT MISUNDERSTANDING

I think that these questions have been greatly misunderstood among God's children. Even though we have talked about this from the beginning, this misunderstanding still continues to exist. Many consider that the requirement on a co-worker is in the matter of finances. Who are the co-workers? Some think that the co-workers are a group of people who have dropped their jobs and fully rely on God. If this is true, then Paul was not our co-worker, because he did not drop his job.

Many consider that an apostle is a person who has no other income or revenue and puts all his time into the work. If he is not so, he is not an apostle. If this concept is true, then Paul definitely would not be an apostle, because Paul did not drop his job altogether. Paul still made tents on the side. If we take the view of God's children today, Paul was not an apostle or a worker, because he did not spend twenty-four hours of his day on the work. He spent some time making tents. Regardless of his purpose in making tents, and regardless of what the income from his making of tents was used for, as long as he made tents, Paul would lose his qualification as a worker and as an apostle. Please remember, however, that this is a basic mistake.

Therefore, I hope that you brothers will be thoroughly clear concerning what God really shows us in His Word as to who an apostle is and who a worker is. Is being an apostle based on one dropping his job? Is being a worker based on whether or not one has a job? Or is being an apostle before God based on something else? You see clearly today that according to tradition and habit in the church, people always consider that being an apostle is based upon the matter of a job. If the question of job and finances is not resolved, one is not an apostle or a worker. I do not know if you have seen this kind of situation. This is today's situation. People always think that an apostle should drop his job entirely and put all of his time into the work. I want the brothers and sisters to see that this mistake is not unreasonable. You may say that it is not a mistake but only a misunderstanding. Many people have not seen thoroughly before God what a worker is and what an apostle is; therefore, they have made this mistake.

APOSTLES TRULY NEEDING TO DROP THEIR JOBS

We know that when John and James were called, they were mending nets. The Lord did tell them to drop their nets and give up their boat to come and follow Him. We also see that when Peter was called, he was fishing. The Lord told him to give up his boat and drop his catch to come and follow Him. When the Lord called Matthew as he was working in the tax office, the Lord told him to leave his job and follow Him. Therefore, let us see clearly before God that an apostle is a person who needs to leave his occupation. According to God's Word, the worker whom God requires must receive a calling before God and give up his job. He needs to put all his time into the hands of the Lord.

This is the fact. If a person has another occupation on the earth, it will be very difficult for him to be an apostle, for an apostle needs to be sent to various places. Even in a place like Jerusalem, the apostles still needed to leave Jerusalem to go to Samaria and Caesarea. Therefore, if one has a job, it would be hard for him to leave, and his work would be restricted to one place.

For this reason, there is no requirement for the elders to drop their jobs, although the apostles provide an example of dropping their jobs. Some elders also need the support from the church. Because they put most or all of their time into church affairs in a local church, they have no income. In such a case, the elders truly should receive double honor. Part of this honor is financial. But requiring the elders to drop their jobs is a different matter. In the Bible there is neither such a command nor such a pattern.

It is not the same with the apostles. The Lord clearly told one to leave this or that behind to come and follow Him, another to put this or that aside to come and follow Him, and another to drop this or that to come and follow Him. This clearly shows us that a person who would be an apostle is one who receives God's command to go to various places. This person should indeed give up his employment; otherwise, he could be an elder but could not be an apostle, since it would indeed be inconvenient to travel to various places to serve the Lord. Therefore, the twelve apostles had such a calling, such a following, such a dropping of things, and such a waiting on the Lord to supply their physical needs. This causes us spontaneously to see that this is the unique way. Here we see clearly that the Lord called the twelve to come forth completely. The Lord called Paul also to come forth completely. Luke, who was with Paul, also came forth completely.

Paul Being a Tentmaker

However, I want to particularly point out that not only was Paul a tentmaker but Aquila and Priscilla were also tentmakers. Luke was even a physician. The Bible shows us that after a person has left his occupation, he is no longer called by the same designation. Luke was a physician, and because the Bible still used that designation, he must have continued his occupation. Peter was a fisherman, but after he gave up his fishing, he was no longer called Peter the fisherman. Matthew was a tax collector, but after he gave up his job as a tax collector, he was no longer called Matthew the tax collector. Luke was a physician. You can see that if he had completely stopped practicing medicine, the Bible would have called him only Luke, not Luke the physician. Do you see this? Luke was practicing medicine and Paul was making tents. Aquila and Priscilla also made tents. Therefore, we have to look into this matter very carefully to see what it really means.

Acts shows us that Paul, Aquila, and Priscilla were all

tentmakers. Because their employment was the same, they lived together. When Paul was in Miletus saying farewell to the elders of Ephesus, he told them to behold his two hands. Let me tell you, this is the most poignant portion of the Bible. For this very reason, I will share with you in a few days that you must touch the spirit in the Bible when you study the Bible. Due to making tents, his hands may have been cut in many places, wounded in many parts, and much skin may have been lost. Therefore, at that time when many overseers and brothers were together, he told them to behold his two hands. Those two hands must have had something worth seeing. Those two hands must have had something which made them different from others'. Those two hands had passed through toil and scratches. They had wounds and scars. Paul did not say at that point that his two hands had done many things and supplied many people. He first told them to behold his two hands. Later, he said that they had supplied many people. He first mentioned his two hands. His hands were different from common, lazy hands, which did no work. Therefore, he could tell them to behold his two hands; they were different from those of the average person.

Later, when he went to Corinth, he again paid attention to this matter. He worked with his own hands to supply the needs of his fellow workers.

Paul's Occupation Being an Apostle, Not Tentmaking

Here I hope the brothers and sisters will be able to see what the actual relationship between an apostle's financial source and his occupation is. When you look at Peter with his company and Paul with his company, you can see a straight way. If you read the Gospels, you cannot see the straight way there, because they contain only half of the matter. What Paul did in the church was a little different or perhaps more advanced. Here you can see that an apostle must leave his job completely. Please remember that in this matter Paul and Peter were the same; Paul also was a person who left his job completely. In reading those ten or more chapters in Acts, who would imagine that Paul was a tentmaker? When I read the book of Acts, my impression is that Paul was an apostle. When I read the book of Acts, I get no impression that Paul was a tentmaker. Perhaps those who make tents consider that Paul was a tentmaker. However, I acknowledge that Paul was an apostle, not a tentmaker. Only those who make tents, whose hearts are in tentmaking, who want to make money in tentmaking, who live in tents, and who pay attention to tents, would, according to their views and judgment, consider Paul to be a tentmaker. But I think that even a very simple believer, a very common believer, would get only one impression while reading Acts, that is, that Paul was an apostle appointed by God. You would not get the impression that Paul was an artisan in making tents. You would not notice that Paul was a tent craftsman. You would see clearly that he was God's worker.

Therefore, as far as the service of an apostle is concerned, one must leave his occupation. However, this refers to a person for whom fishing is an occupation. The man who needs to leave the occupation of tax collecting is the one for whom tax collecting is an occupation. The man who needs to leave the craft of tentmaking is the one for whom tentmaking is an occupation. If tentmaking was an occupation, then this occupation had to be left behind. If it was not left behind, one could not be an apostle, because the service of the apostle would be rather difficult for him. Why does God require people to leave their occupations in order to be an apostle? It is because apostleship is an occupation, and a person cannot have two occupations. In particular, the occupation of an apostle does not allow a person to take a second job. Paul said that we are ambassadors of Christ. If we are ambassadors, we have no way to take a second job and no way to have another occupation. All of our time is for working as an apostle; we have no time to spend on other matters.

Therefore, Paul's tentmaking was not an occupation; the tentmaking of Aquila and Priscilla was not an occupation either. Even Luke's being a physician was not an occupation.

The Situation in Those Days Being Different

What do we see here? We see that Paul was sent by the

Holy Spirit to go out from Antioch and travel to various places
to work. There is a great difference between the situation
today and the situation in those days in the matter of
transportation. In those days, if the brothers in Antioch had
some money and material things to give to Paul, they could
not go to the post office to remit the money. Neither was
there a bank, express air mail, or telegrams. In the New
Testament there are quite a few cases in which gifts were
sent in person. Paul himself did this when he was in Antioch.
The first time he went out was not for gospel preaching but
to carry money to Jerusalem. I often think that our doing
such things could be uplifted—first you send money and later
you go out to preach the gospel. The first time he carried
money to Jerusalem as an ambassador of the church. Later,
when Paul received gifts, they were carried to him by people
sent from various churches. You see how difficult it was
without letters, telegrams, and airplanes. All those who went
out for the gospel took nothing from the Gentiles. The apostle
Paul was different from the apostles in Jerusalem.

To go out from Jerusalem did not take long, and the
journey was short. One could return in a short time and
have no financial difficulty because he could take sufficient
money for the trip to Samaria and Caesarea and return
after a period of time without needing to take anything
from the Gentiles. This was easy because both Caesarea and
Samaria were localities with churches. Later, Paul's work
started from Antioch, and God gave him another way. The
way was for him to go to the Gentiles, yet take nothing
from the Gentiles, and continue to go out, not returning in
a short period of time like the apostles in Jerusalem. He
kept going from place to place. Therefore, we can see that
the matter of support was very difficult. One could not take
enough money along, and neither could one take anything
from the Gentiles.

This is also different from the gospel preaching in the
Gospels. In the Gospels one went to the cities and lived in
the house of a generous man. One did not need to bring his
staff or his purse. However, when the Lord was about to
depart from the earth, He told His disciples that he who did

not have a staff needed to bring a staff, he who had no purse should prepare a purse, and he who had no clothes needed to prepare clothing. The situation had become different. The gospel was not to be preached to Jews but to Gentiles. John made it very clear that we should take nothing from the Gentiles. Therefore, we can see how heavy the burden on Paul was at that time, not only for himself, but also for the brothers who were together with him.

When they started out from Antioch, there was only Barnabas and Paul. Later, when they went out, there were others who went with them, one of whom was Titus. On the way Timothy was added, Luke was added, and later Silas was also added. As they went, the company became larger, and the further they went, the more the number of people increased. Later, Priscilla and Aquila also came along. They preached the gospel along the way in locality after locality. Then Paul said that he worked with his own hands to supply his own needs and the needs of his co-workers. Let me tell you, this was not a matter of occupation; his occupation was apostle. But when there was the need along the way, he personally worked with his own hands to provide the support for himself and for those who were with him.

This was a very good thing. Alford tells us that in those days, in order to make a tent, you needed to use a certain dye to color the tent material. The dye was very strong, and the color did not easily fade. When a hand was corroded by the dye, the skin would be damaged. Therefore, Paul could tell the Ephesians to behold his two hands. This was a very great matter. Therefore, I hope the brothers could see the financial problem of the apostles: If various churches can send support, thank God; but if various churches cannot send support, it does not mean that we should take other occupations or change our occupation as apostles. This is the problem today. Our occupation is as apostles. But I may make tents today in order to have this occupation. Today, in order that I and the brothers with me can be apostles, I may make tents. Making tents was not Paul's occupation. Paul's occupation never changed. From the time he was called in Damascus, his occupation never changed. In order that the

young men who were with him could have a supply, he made
tents. Because he knew how, Paul made tents with his own
hands when Timothy, Titus, Silas, and Luke were with him,
to supply their needs. Behold, these two hands!

Making Tents so that He Could Be an Apostle

Therefore, we see here that apostles truly need to leave
their own occupations. Apostles also need to have only one
occupation, which is the occupation of being an apostle. But
I want to mention Paul to clarify this one matter. This does
not mean that he could not go and make some money. Paul
was an apostle, and he always worked as an apostle. When
we read the book of Acts, we would never dream that Paul
changed his line of work. Paul went to Ephesus and made
tents, yet he was still an apostle, and in Ephesus especially
he made many more tents so that he could experience the
church life. Whether one made tents or practiced medicine,
all were for the purpose of being an apostle, not that he
might not be an apostle. Perhaps he could not be an apostle
if he did not make tents. I hope we can see this point clearly
before God. Many times, God allowed Paul to do some work
to enable Paul to be an apostle all the more.

Do we see this? This is a matter entirely different from
occupation. This is entirely different from what we ordinarily
call occupation. Today, if Matthew would go back to be a
tax collector, we would say that Matthew was looking for a
job. But, today if Paul would go to make tents, we would
not say that Paul was looking for a job. Matthew could not
say that he must be a tax collector in order to be an apostle.
However, Paul could say, "Behold, these two hands! Without
them, it seems that I cannot be an apostle." His tentmaking
enabled him to be an apostle all the more. His purpose was
to be an apostle, his living was as an apostle, his work was
as an apostle, and his life was as an apostle; all that he
was, was as an apostle. His two hands helped him to be an
apostle. His two hands did not distract him so that he could
not be an apostle. Brothers, is this clear? This way is very
clear.

The Question of a Second Job

A certain brother asked me a month or two ago whether we should give up our occupation completely or take a second job in the future, if we go out to preach the gospel for the Lord and do the work of an apostle. I tell you, this is my answer today. Everyone who wants to be an apostle must throw away his occupation, throw away what man calls occupation. However, please note that while you travel to various places for the gospel, it would be better to take a second job to enable you to be an apostle rather than complain that the church lacks love, as some do because of their own lack of faith. Rather than being weak in faith and maintaining hope toward God in appearance, but in reality having hope toward man and the brothers, it would be better to be like Paul and say, "These hands!" It would be better at that time to work a little with your own hands so that you could support yourself and also support others. I think and believe that the most dishonorable thing to God is to look to the love of the church more than having faith before God. I think and I believe that the most dishonorable thing to God is to complain against men, yet not be able to trust in the Lord. I think it is more dishonorable to God for a man to hope in God in appearance, yet in reality to turn his eyes not heavenward but toward his surroundings and environment. This is even more dishonorable to God.

The Principle of "These Hands!"

However, here is a matter which I would do my best to emphasize—the principle of "These hands!", that is, that these two hands will enable me to be an apostle all the more. The two hands of many people do not need to fish. Do we see this? We must emphatically maintain before God what we are really doing, what we are here for on this earth, and what kind of persons we are before God. Please remember that before God you are an apostle called by God. Because you are an apostle, you must leave your occupation entirely. From now on, even if you work with your hands again, it is not for an occupation. If you work with your hands again, it is to supply you and the needs of your fellow workers. There are needs because you are an apostle. You have become an apostle; therefore, there are needs, and you must work with your hands. My brothers here have needs; therefore, I need to work with my hands so that they can be apostles. I work with my hands in the hope that I may support myself and my co-workers, not because of a lack in my own finances, or because I am hindered, or because I have taken a wrong way.

Therefore, I hope the brothers and sisters can see that this way is different. It is not a change of occupation, but the support of our apostleship with a job. It is not changing from apostleship to the occupation of tentmaking, but supporting our apostleship by the work of tentmaking.

Fishing and Tentmaking Being Two Different Matters

If a brother thinks that he cannot do the work well or that he has financial difficulties, he may go to teach or to fish. I tell you that when the Lord died, many did go fishing. But, when the Lord died, could you say that our Lord was living forever in the heavens? Only the disappointed ones went fishing! But here was a person who went to make tents not out of disappointment; there was no disappointment at all. These are two different matters.

Peter's fishing and Paul's tentmaking were two entirely different matters. Peter's fishing was his arriving at a dead end with no way to go on. Peter's fishing meant that he considered the Lord to have died, to be finished, to be terminated, and that everything was hopeless. He considered himself as a failure, and the Lord had died; therefore, he went fishing. Brothers, you must take note that Paul's tentmaking was not an occupation. Paul had clearly determined that the Lord was living, and he could not help but be an apostle. If it was comfortable, he would be an apostle, and if it was a suffering, he would still be an apostle. If he received money, he would be an apostle, and if he did not receive any money, he would still be an apostle. When there was the support from the brothers, he would be an apostle, and when there was no support, he would still be an apostle.

This is an entirely different matter from Peter's fishing. To live was to be an apostle, and to die was also to be an apostle. If he needed to endeavor, he would still endeavor to be an apostle. He put his two hands to it; besides all the work and all the labor, he was willing to do one more work so that the work of the apostles would not collapse. This was Paul. He was this way not only toward himself, but also toward those who were with him. By the work of his two hands he supported himself and also those who were with him. This was the way in which Paul walked.

Not Changing Occupations but Endeavoring All the More

Today, brothers and sisters, we need to see this basic principle: All who go out to preach the gospel, who have been called by the Lord to serve Him fully in the gospel, who are apostles, whether brothers or sisters, need to throw away their occupation entirely. This is the proper way. We should drop everything to be an apostle. However, when there is the need and if we can bear the extra burden to work for a short period of time, then we may work, but not as the tax collectors who work day and night in the tax office. If there is no such need, then we do not have to work. When the church has no way to support or when the church does not support, as in the days when the Israelites did not give the offerings and the Levites were hungry, we may work a little on the side to help ourselves and our co-workers and still be an apostle. Please remember, the principle of tentmaking not only does not distract us, but it makes us single-hearted all the more. Not only is it not a hindrance, but rather it is a help. Not only is it not the changing of our occupation, but rather it is the bettering of our occupation. Brothers and sisters, this means we need to endeavor all the more. We have to bear the work which the Lord has assigned to us and the responsibility which the Lord has given to us. Because we want to bear it, we will use all our means to bear it. It is right to go out to work in this way. This I say in reference to the apostles specifically.

THE SCOPE OF THE DEFINITION OF A CO-WORKER
BEING WIDER THAN THAT OF AN APOSTLE

What about the co-workers? The scope of the definition of a co-worker is actually wider than that of an apostle. Aquila and Priscilla were both co-workers. Phoebe was a co-worker. The responsible elders and deacons in every church were also co-workers.

Requiring the Occupation of Every Person to Be Secondary

We would ask all the brothers and sisters to change their occupation into a secondary occupation. It is good, even very good, if in your locality you have the means to support yourself and you completely give up your occupation simply to serve God in your locality. It is also good if in this locality you serve God, bear the local responsibility with the ministry of the word, or take part in the office or in the service, while doing something to support yourself and others. I do not know whether or not you have seen this. Among us no brother or sister lives for himself. No brother or sister fishes for himself. Among us all the brothers and sisters fish for their office or their service. If this is the case, the problem of occupation can be resolved very easily. If you are clear concerning your office, then you will be clear about your occupation. If you are not clear about your office or service, let me say that your occupation will be absolutely useless before God.

The Purpose Being for Service

A certain brother asked me if it is good to have a second job. At that time I answered that it is good and that it is all right to take up a second job. But this is not the question. The question is what is your primary work. Before God a person must have an intention and a purpose. Paul said that his intention, his desire, or we may say, ambition, and goal were to please the Lord. What was his purpose and ambition? He said, "To gain the honor of being well pleasing to Him" (2 Cor. 5:9). The first question you need to answer today is, "Why are you doing business?" Is it to earn money or to be rich? Some people want to become rich and not just earn money. Even many physicians in Shanghai are not simply for earning money but for becoming rich. Our purpose before God is not to become rich, but to earn money, to have a little income, and to support the Lord's work. This foundation must be established first. You must make a decision within yourself as to what you really want before the Lord. Paul said he wanted to please the Lord. What do you want? Today before the Lord I have only one purpose: I want to serve Him, and I want His work to be done well.

Occupation Being a Minor Issue

Today all the brothers and sisters must deal with this issue—we must give all to serve the Lord. I tell you, if we do so, the matter of occupation is a small thing. What you do is a small thing. If you are not strong before the Lord and your service to God is not strong, your situation is like a work of silk weaving which cannot be touched without rending it. Once you touch it, there will be a tear. If before the Lord your service to Him is strong, even if you go back to work, the way is still open. Perhaps certain brothers may return to be physicians, to embroider, or to make hair nets. But if this is something you do on the side in order to support your service, there is no problem. This will not cause a problem for your ministry, because you are not in that occupation.

For example, soon our brothers will go back to take care of a linen or embroidery business. They are prepared to sell the product in order to use all that they have to support their office before God. Their function before God is so pressing and critical that everything else they do is to help their function. Again, there may be a person who has a hair net or embroidery business. He has set his heart and mind to become rich, yet he says, "I am the same as the other brothers. Because I want to be rich, I assume that the other brothers also desire to be rich and that there is no difference between us." I tell you, before God his way is wrong, and the carrying out of his office will be restricted. His purpose is to become rich, but our purpose is not to become rich. All occupations can be carried out in the same manner, but our way is for serving God.

Serving God in Whatever We Do

If I want to serve God, I must serve God in whatever I do.
You have to give all to this. Not only not making tents is for
being an apostle, but even making tents is for being an apostle.
Not only not fishing is for being an apostle, but even fishing
is for being an apostle. Therefore, I hope none of the brothers
who are apostles would change their priority before God. I
also hope that none of the brothers who are serving God in
the localities would change their priorities either. Serving God
is our career, our basic career. Whatever I do is for serving
God. Not making money is to serve God, and making money
is also to serve God. Designating a certain portion of my
time is also for serving God. If I walk in this way without an
obstacle, I am serving God. If I walk in this way, find an
obstacle, and change my means of walking, I am also serving
God. I would even give my life. Thus, the issue is settled.

All Those Who Are for the Lord
Being Co-Workers

All those who are for the Lord are our co-workers.
Brothers, do you see this? This is because our primary office
is the same. Before God, all the brothers are for serving the
Lord. We can say before the Lord that these are our
co-workers, as Paul said in Romans 16:3, "my fellow workers."
All who serve the Lord have become our co-workers. Please
remember therefore that the matter of co-workers is not as
we previously thought. Someone may give twenty-four hours
a day and still not be our co-worker. Then again, a person
may work only two hours every night, yet we can say that
this brother is our co-worker. Whether or not one is a
co-worker does not depend on having a job or on finances.
Whether or not one is a co-worker depends on how much the
work occupies him. A person may wash laundry or clean floors
and still be our co-worker. A person can weave cloth or repair
clothes and still be our co-worker. It does not matter what
work he does. A person may work on a locomotive or on a
ship—water and fire are not the same, and land and sea are
not the same—but he is still a co-worker. One brother may

go back to his linen business, and another brother may go back to practice medicine. If our purpose of serving God so that He may have a way in China is the same, if you give your all and I also give my all, if you give all your time and I also give my time, if you give all your money and I give all my money, I tell you, we are co-workers. We are not only co-workers with one another; we are co-workers with Peter and Paul as well. We are co-workers with those who have served God for these many years.

The Work Not Being the Same
but the Purpose Being the Same

Today many people have a mistaken view, paying attention to being the same in work, rather than in purpose. Many do not pay attention to how strong or how critical the purpose is, but rather to whether or not things are the same. Please remember that for things to be the same does not make you co-workers. Perhaps when a brother goes to Tsingtao, he can find five or ten doctors there. They may be working with him in the same clinic, but you cannot say that they are our co-workers. The jobs are the same, but they are not our co-workers. There is only one thing—I live here to help in the gospel, and all my income is for the gospel. I tell you, this settles all the issues.

For example, a doctor, who has a noble occupation, and a sister who washes laundry may still be co-workers. One of them has studied for many years and received years of fine training, whereas the other has little education, but because their purpose is the same, they are co-workers. Another Christian may have received the same education, yet not be a co-worker.

If you endeavor with all that you have, you have a way. Brothers, this is the main, basic, and chief thing. Therefore, brothers and sisters, I often feel that if someone is absolutely for the Lord, gives everything he has, does not care for the world, lives on the earth wholly for the Lord, and uses all his means whatever they may be to serve God, regardless of what job he has and regardless of his position, you will feel that he is a person full of light.

Needing to Serve By All Means

I tell you, there are not many co-workers, and there have never been many. We ask God that He would indeed do the work of recovery in these last days and that many would have such a heart to serve the Lord by all means. For this reason, I appreciate those two hands of Paul. According to the proper way, many things need not have been done. As a rule, the church should be responsible for the entire support of the work and all the needs of the apostles. However, the church did not bear the responsibility. When the church failed to bear the responsibility and only cared for its own needs, when it forgot the support for Paul, and not only did not support him, but even criticized him, he said, "These hands!" Therefore, I hope you can see that all these things did not diminish his apostleship, but they even established, supported, and strengthened his apostleship. His apostleship depended on his two hands. In other words, these two exceptional hands, these hands which should not have worked for support, were not needed when the church was on the proper way. However, Paul was willing. Therefore, I say very frankly, that this is to serve by all means. As long as we can serve, it is good. We must always serve.

Therefore, today I think that we first must settle the issue of who a co-worker is. We naturally have a mistaken thought, thinking that co-workers are those who have given up their occupation and have income other than that which comes from an occupation. This is not so. Co-workers are those who have one heart, one purpose, and one ambition before God and who are serving God to please Him. As long as their purpose is the same, these are all co-workers in the Lord, no matter what jobs their hands are engaged in.

Chapter Twelve

THE MATTER OF FINANCES

Now we want to talk about what kind of arrangements we should have in our midst in the matter of finances. On the one hand, how should we distribute the income of the church? On the other hand, what should the relationship be among the co-workers?

THE DISTRIBUTION OF MONEY IN A LOCAL CHURCH

Normal Expenses

Regarding the question of money, I think it will be clearer if I speak in this way: The income of the local church is first, of course, for local expenses. A locality should not be in debt. In the local church there are many expenditures. First, there are the normal expenses of the church, such as the wine, the bread, electricity, water, and in some places, rent.

Taking Care of the Poor

Second, there are certain matters that the local churches need to devote more effort to. In the church God especially stresses that His children should take care of the needy, especially the needy brothers. Therefore, in the local church there is a major need of taking care of the needy brothers.

But when we take care of the needy brothers, we should do it very carefully. We cannot say that because they are needy brothers, we can be discourteous to them. When brothers send money to them, we should not cause them to feel ashamed just because they are needy. If we have an elderly mother and father at home, the way we send money to them is the way I hope that we would take care of the poor. It should be just as if we were sending money to our elderly parents. We certainly cannot let our parents feel that their son is having pity on them or that their son is giving them charity to relieve them of their difficulties. We cannot do it this way. In the church when we are managing money to care for the needy, we should be very skillful. In every church the brothers and sisters who pass on money must be people with keen feelings; we cannot send insensitive persons. Needy ones cannot help but receive our money, but they also could not help but be hurt. Therefore, there is a need for people with keen feelings. We should never allow anyone to hurt them.

For example, suppose a brother fell and was injured and we needed to carry him to his bed. We would never send clumsy, insensitive persons to do it. Maybe a bone was not broken, but because they are clumsy, they can break a bone. I feel in many places that the brothers who manage money are too insensitive in their feeling. I am not happy about this situation at all. Sooner or later those people may fall into a condition of great poverty before God; definitely God will place some discipline on them. How could they be without any feeling at all? When a brother or sister is in difficulty, we need to be very tender in helping this one. In every locality, regarding the question of money, one part is for the expenses of the church, and one part is for taking care of the needs of the brothers. We need to select a brother who is especially gentle, whose feeling is especially keen, one who can sense the situation from just one word. Such a one should be asked to handle these affairs. If it is not so, problems will arise. We need to be very tender, very fine, very careful. We should not allow these brothers to feel that they are giving charity.

Let me relate one incident to you. Here in Kuling there are a few terms which are quite peculiar. For example, when they want to say "intend" or "plan," they use the term *continue.* Similarly, to help someone is "to favor them." No matter what they use to help people with, they say that it is "to favor them." More than a month ago, when I was going down the mountain, a few of the sedan-chair bearers told me, "Mr. Nee, I really favor you; I really favor you." I said, "What do you mean?" They said, "Every time that you call us to bear the sedan-chair, we always respond very quickly because we really favor you." I hope that in helping the needy ones, we do not do it in the way of favoring them. This is ugly. When you go to help them, never give the appearance that you are doing them a favor. When a believer is in a time of difficulty, you need to preserve his self-respect and his dignity. You do not know when you will be in the same situation. Never do anything to hurt him. This needs to be handled very delicately.

Taking Care of the Needs
of the Responsible Brothers

Third, there is another thing that the local church can do. If a local responsible brother spends all of his time in the affairs of the church and it causes his own job or business to suffer, the church should give him financial help in a very careful way. You are aware that there are many brothers in the local church, especially responsible brothers, who, because of being busy with many church affairs, were unable to continue on with their business and lost their source of income. Due to being occupied with the church, they laid aside their work. This is the situation mentioned in the book of Timothy, where some are worthy of double honor. You should not just send money to the brothers who are workers and neglect the responsible brothers. For a responsible brother to spend all of his time in a church in his locality and suffer is not right. The local church should learn to take care of the needs of the responsible brothers.

Sending Financial Help
to Other Local Churches for Their Use

In addition, a local church can also send money to other local churches for their use. Many local churches may have difficulties. Sometimes there are particular hardships, as in the case of Antioch sending money to Jerusalem. When the brothers in Jerusalem had difficulties, the brothers in Antioch sent money to Jerusalem. This is also something that a local church should do. We may hear of special circumstances in a church in a certain locality. As a consequence, we should send them money. The mutual supply among the churches is an important matter. Remember that in the beginning in Jerusalem, many brothers and sisters sold their lands and houses. During the time of famine, Antioch sent money through the hand of Barnabas and Paul. I am glad that the elders in Antioch did not ask, "We wonder whether they have spent all that money. Do the apostles still have anything left over from that sale?" This was not something the other churches did. What was done in Acts was very good. Antioch rose up and sent brothers to take money to Jerusalem to supply the need in Jerusalem. It was at this time that Barnabas came from Jerusalem to Antioch for the purpose of helping Antioch, and Antioch asked Barnabas to take the money and go and help Jerusalem. This is a very pleasant thing.

Giving to Individual Workers

There is another matter. When a local church receives income, there should be money given to individual workers. This is what Philippi did with Paul. When Paul was working in the region of Macedonia and in Thessalonica, the church in Philippi once and again sent money for his use. When we read the book of Philippians, we know that when Paul was in Macedonia and Thessalonica, all of his money came from Philippi. Otherwise, the work could not have gone on. Therefore, we need to help the brothers everywhere to see and help them to learn to give money to the brothers who are workers. The church in Corinth was à declining church; its spiritual condition before God was poor. With respect to the supplying of Paul, they only criticized. Nothing was given. They gave Paul nothing except criticism. Therefore, I think that the churches in various localities should pay attention to how to give money to those who serve the Lord. The churches should pay attention to the aspect of giving to individuals.

Giving to the Work in the Region

I want the brothers and sisters to pay attention to yet another need. The money from all the local churches should be sent not only to the individual workers, but also to the work in the entire region. If our view is not mistaken, the exhortation that Paul gave to the Corinthians was that he expected them to prepare the money to be sent to Jerusalem. At that time there was not just one church that sent money to Jerusalem; the churches in Galatia sent money as well. Galatia is a province, and there were many churches there. Paul exhorted the church in Corinth to gather their money and send it quickly to Jerusalem, just as the churches in Galatia had done. At that time not only was Jerusalem in famine, but Judea was as well. Hence, the money sent to Jerusalem was given not only for the local church in Jerusalem, but also for Judea, the entire region represented by Jerusalem. The money was sent to Jerusalem so that Jerusalem could send it to all of Judea. There is a principle here. Money can be given to a local church for their use. For example, if Foochow is in difficulty, we can give money to the local church in Foochow. If Wenchow has problems, we can send money to the local church in Wenchow. However, if that region has difficulties, then the money would not be given to the one locality of Foochow, but Foochow should be asked to make arrangements for distribution to the brothers and sisters in the entire region. Therefore, we should show the churches that with respect to the work among the churches, there is this matter of region. If a church in a region is having difficulties, the brothers should learn to give.

Even during normal times when the churches are not in difficulty and there are many co-workers in a region, everyone should learn before God to pay attention to the need of all of the co-workers in the region. The local churches need to learn to send the money to the co-workers in the region so that they can distribute it among the co-workers in that region.

I do not know if you are clear that these are things that a local church should do concerning money. What they have received, they need to use for local expenses, for needy brothers, for the responsible brothers, for brothers in the work in other cities, for the needs of other churches, and for the region.

THE RELATIONSHIP AMONG CO-WORKERS
The Need for Those Taking the Lead
to Care for the Co-workers

I especially want to mention another point. There are persons such as Paul who bear considerable responsibility but are not from a particular locality. Timothy, Titus, Silas, and Luke were known to the churches only in later times, but not in the beginning. All those who are in the position of Paul need to learn the principle that "these hands have ministered to my needs and to those who are with me" (Acts 20:34). No brother can be a leader in the work and yet be miserly in matters of money. In China I know two or three brothers who were quite useful in God's hands in the beginning, and yet they cannot be conceived of as leaders among the brothers in the matter of money. They were only able to receive. They were only able to live by faith, but they did not know how to give by faith. Therefore, before the Lord, they never had a way to lead other servants of God to go forward. I also knew a sister who had a deep knowledge of God. She was very godly and could lead people, but she did not have the faith to supply others. Those who are learning to be like Paul may not have attained to Paul's standing, but if their names are especially known to the churches, they need to care for those whose names are not known to the churches. You need to know that your income is not just for you alone but also for those who are with you. If you keep the income for yourself, a time will come when you will be manifested to be unworthy to lead your co-workers. If you cause those younger co-workers to receive less money than you, what shall they do? This is clearly a failure of those who would stand in the position of Paul.

Therefore, all those who are the leaders among the co-workers in various localities and who are known to the churches must have the habit of giving, especially giving to those who are with them. You have to see that the Lord's supply to you is not just for you personally, but also for your co-workers. As long as the money is held tightly in your hands, you will be put outside of your work sooner or later. The gifts

that God has given you cannot replace the gifts that you give
to others. If you are foolish, you will think that since God
gave to you, you are able to serve the church. This is wrong.
You need to give to others; then you can serve the church.
Therefore, I hope that the brothers who are like Paul would
learn to give to other brothers so that they can have a proper
living. The elderly brothers in every locality should also learn
to give to their co-workers from the offerings they receive. Do
not care just for your own needs but for those of your
co-workers as well.

Distributing according to Everyone's Need

How should a brother who is a leading one distribute
money to his co-workers? Suppose a brother has eight or ten
co-workers in Canton. How should he distribute money to
them? I think that the principle in the Bible is to give
according to each one's need and not according to each one's
gift. Many times the brothers in the church give money to a
brother because of his gift in the work. We cannot support
a brother who is useful in the work according to his spiritual
gift; we have to support him according to his need. The
brothers may be wrong, but we should not be wrong, because
we are leading ones in the work. Therefore, we should be
more knowledgeable than they.

For this reason, in normal times the brothers who bear
responsibility in the work should make a list of the brothers
in the work in their area. This does not mean that they have
something formal, but rather that the responsible brothers
need to have the number. They need to have a list of names,
including the number of their children and how many are in
school. There is a difference between a single person and one
with children. We cannot make arrangements on a moment's
notice. We know that the burdens of some brothers are light,
those of some brothers are heavy, and those of others are
very heavy. If we have such a list in our hands, then when
money is put into our hands for the work in our region, we
will know how to support them according to their need. This
does not mean that there is something formal among us. But
the responsible brothers should learn to be aware of how

many brothers are in the work in this region and how great
their needs are. When money comes into our hands, we can
then distribute according to our own needs and their needs.

At one time in Foochow, I helped a brother compile a list
of the co-workers in that region. In Shanghai I also helped
a brother do this. My point is that the needs of many brothers
can be met by doing this.

The Need to Look to God and
Our Not Bearing the Responsibility for Anyone

However, if the Lord does not send money, we still have
to look to God. We cannot bear the responsibility for anyone.
No one bears the responsibility for us, and neither can we
bear the responsibility for them. But when there is money to
distribute, it is not according to one's ministry, but according
to one's need. In this way meeting the needs of the co-workers
will be with equality. We cannot give to them formally; they
themselves have to learn to look to God. Other churches or
brothers from different localities can give to them on their
own. When we have extra, we can distribute it to those who
are with us in that region. When there is income in our
region, we can distribute it according to the need. I hope that
we can take care of the financial matters properly among us.
God will gain the glory in this matter.

QUESTIONS

The Practical Way to Distribute

Arrangements Being Needed

Question: How should we distribute money in the local
church at the center of the work? There we have both elders
and co-workers, and some of the elders need to be in the
distribution. How should the distribution be carried out
practically?

Answer: It is a matter of the arrangement that we
mentioned earlier. Although it is not something formal, there
need to be some decisions. If there is an additional need, we
must look to God. Why did I help the brothers in Foochow
and Shanghai make their arrangements? It was because it

was more convenient for us to bear this responsibility. Even though I do not have the time, I still did it because it was more convenient for me to do it. Naturally, if they were to do it, they would feel that it was awkward.

After Expenditures and Gifts, the Remainder Being Sent to Other Localities

The distribution of money in a local church should always be for local expenditures first. Canton, for example, may receive one thousand dollars every month. The first responsibility of a local church is to take care of the local expenditures and the needy brothers. The needs of the elders can often be included with the needs of the co-workers. At the same time, according to the principle, the money which a local church receives should be sent to other localities.

This is because as soon as a local church keeps money for its own use, many problems will arise and many improper principles will be introduced. In the future difficulties may arise among us, although I do not mean that this could happen today. We need to remember the situation in Rome. In Rome the situation became such that the Romish apostles would go out only to those localities where there would be an income; if there was no income, the Romish apostles would not go there. At that time the situation in Rome had actually developed to this extent. In England, whenever a pastor goes to a place to be a pastor or an overseer, he will say, "I am called to" a certain place. Amazingly, many are called to wealthy places, but no one is called to impoverished places, and everything of the world follows them. This is very ugly and absolutely not spiritual. Worldly thoughts and thoughts of money came into the church.

I have considered this matter much before God. You can see that at the beginning in Antioch Paul was one who carried money. There was no mention at all of the need in Antioch or of the need of the work in Antioch; Paul only carried money to Jerusalem. Later, the region of Achaia sent money to Jerusalem, the region of Galatia sent money to Jerusalem, and the area around Corinth also sent money to Jerusalem. At that time there could have been the misunderstanding that

Paul's tentmaking business was prosperous and that he did not need more money. Therefore, I believe that when we manage money in our region, the best way is not to let the local co-workers have it but to always send it to other places. Our needs will be met with what comes from other places. We prefer to let the bank earn a service fee for sending the money. We have to put the church on spiritual ground. As soon as our ground is not spiritual, we are useless.

Today in China the work must begin in several regions. All of the brothers in a region should endeavor to consider the work in other regions. What Paul did was very comely. He went out from Antioch and brought money to Jerusalem. He entreated Galatia, Corinth, and the whole region of Achaia to send money to Jerusalem. It seemed that while there were needs on every side, he personally did not have any need at all. Actually, his two hands did not cease to work. We have seen how he said to the Ephesians, "These hands!" Man always thinks that his needs come first, regardless of everything else. I hope that we will care for the need in other places and let our needs be cared for by God. God will lead brothers to care for our personal needs. Our way is to believe in the sovereignty of the Holy Spirit. The entire Bible shows us that God has His arrangement in everything. We believe in the arrangement of the Holy Spirit. Therefore, if I have an extraordinary need today, I can look only to God to grant me a special miracle. Then a brother may suddenly meet my need and resolve my difficulty. God is living!

Furthermore, I do not want there to be a dead method in the region. I fear formal things. I believe that the brothers who have been with me for so many years all know that I fear formal things, because once something becomes formal, it ceases to be spiritual. However, I want you to keep the following principle. If in the region of Canton you have some income, at the most you should keep a portion of it, perhaps one-third or two-fifths, always less than half, and designate the greater part to be sent to other localities. Presently, we have ten regions of work. We do not send the same amount to each one. You yourselves have to receive the leading before God.

In this way God will easily maintain the support in the church. Please remember that as soon as the Israelites ceased to provide, the Levites went hungry. For the Levites to have a problem indicated that Israel had a problem. For the Levites to have no lack was a proof that the Israelites were standing on God's side. Therefore, we need to learn to send money to other localities to care for their work. As for us, we need to let God spontaneously maintain the work in our locality.

The advantage to this is that the locality which has the supply will not have too much, and the locality which does not have the supply will not have too much lack.

When responsible brothers or co-workers have a need, we should make some arrangements. We need to see what the magnitude of their need is and give to them proportionately. Then we will not have troubling thoughts. In this way I believe that many problems will pass away, and that we will avoid many troubles. Otherwise, how are we going to apportion the money in a local church? It will be very troublesome. Who would then give money to a responsible brother? Being a responsible brother in that locality, how could one take the money himself? Who would give it to him? His sense as a Christian would not allow him to take it. Therefore, we must make arrangements for him to spare him this inconvenience.

The Need to Have Two to Handle the Money

I personally believe that in every region there should be at least two persons to handle the money. The principle in the Bible is always to have two. The first time it was Barnabas and Paul. Subsequently, there were always two persons. We need two brothers to handle the money and manage the accounts. Perhaps one brother will handle decision making in particular, and one brother will mainly take care of the bookkeeping.

The Need for the Ledger to Be Public

Question: Some churches publicly display the ledger, while other places do not. What should the principle be?

Answer: I think that the income of a local church should

be displayed. Matters related to the work should be known to the co-working brothers and sisters of the region.

First the Expenses, Then the Apostles

Question: Because many people do not know how to give an offering, should the offering boxes be separately designated for the locality and for the work?

Answer: It does not matter if the brothers and sisters do not designate them; we have to do the designating. The expenses of a local church, such as electricity, water, and rent, should always come first. The needy brothers come second. The workers should always be placed third and not first. If we are first, then something is wrong. Therefore, we need to care for the needy brothers first. This is a basic principle. The church in Jerusalem gave first to the brothers in need, not to the co-workers. Therefore, workers should not be mistaken to think that the apostles are first. On the contrary, the poor, the needy brothers, the widows, and the orphans are first. We need to help these people first, then come to the apostles. We should never first care for the apostles, then care for the poor. That would be completely backwards. The case in Jerusalem is quite clear: The offerings were distributed among all according as anyone had need. After this come the responsible brothers. We do not want to be the first.

This is also done according to the spiritual principle. First, we send money out, then money will be sent to us from outside. We should retain a small amount, whether one-third, one-fifth, or one-tenth, the less the better. The rest should always be sent out. In this way there will be no problems.

When we do have the money, divide it according to the need. Do it according to the proportions we have written down. If we personally have a particular need, then we should go before God separately and look to Him for the need. Co-workers can receive only according to their proportion. I think this closely follows the biblical principle. The matter of money is a very difficult matter, but I think that handling it this way is very much according to the Bible. Based on what I can see in Acts and the Epistles in the New Testament, there is only this principle. The method used to divide money was very good. There was no difficulty at all; it was divided in a very good way. "These hands have ministered to my needs and to those who are with me." This is a matter of need, not gift. A church might say that since a certain brother is able to preach, they would give him more. I cannot give more to Timothy because he preaches better than Titus. The word *need* is very good; with it we cannot easily go wrong.

The Way to Distribute Money Entrusted to You

Question: If someone entrusts me with the distribution of an amount of money, how should I determine the proportions?

Answer: Before a list of proportions is produced, according to my personal view, I myself would not use anything that has been entrusted to me for distribution. As soon as I use any, there will be a problem. As soon as you use it, spontaneously you will appear to be unfaithful. No matter how clear your conscience is, you still will not be at peace. A difficulty with the conscience is different from other difficulties; you cannot reason with it. It is like a child that cries when he wants to cry and throws a tantrum when he wants to throw a tantrum. If there is a sum of money for me to distribute, even if I use one dollar, my conscience will have no peace. If it was designated for me, then I can use it as I please. If it is one thousand dollars, it would not matter if I used nine hundred ninety-nine for myself. But if I was asked to administrate and distribute it, I would still give out the whole amount. I believe that once we establish the proportions, we cannot go wrong. In the past we did not have established proportions; we needed to give away the whole amount. In your region every co-worker has a portion due him, and you also have a portion due you. In such a case we should distribute according to the proportions, and no difficulties with the conscience will arise. In the past we indeed gave out the entire amount.

Sometimes a brother or sister sent in money, and when there was no way to distribute it, I wrote a letter telling them that I did not know how to distribute it and asked them what I should do with it. One sister replied with a good answer.

She said, "If you want to throw it into the Whampoa River, that is your business. You can do as you see fit." Because she washed her hands of the affair, it became an entirely different matter.

Sending Letters to All the Places concerning the Building of a Meeting Hall

Question: In the past there were a few localities which wrote to all the other localities when they needed to build meeting halls. Is this a good practice?

Answer: It is not so good. Whenever this kind of letter reaches my desk, I read only the first six words, and then throw it into the wastepaper basket without reading the rest. If an individual brother fellowships with certain brothers in other places, that is all right, because that is not something formal. As soon as this kind of thing becomes formal, I am afraid that it is spoiled.

The Matter of Supporting the Responsible Brothers

Question: The responsible brothers should receive double honor. This is correct, but how should we make it known? It is difficult. If we ask the apostles to decide, that will also be hard. Whenever an apostle goes to a certain place, can we ask him to make an effort to mention that the elders should receive double honor?

Answer: This is a special question concerning the center of the work, not concerning a local church. The list should be only in localities where there is a center of the work.

Timothy Being the One Who Should Speak

According to the letter written by Paul to Timothy, it is very clear that Timothy was the one who should spread the word to the churches in all the localities regarding how a local church distributes money. When workers go to the local churches, they need to tell the brothers in the local churches to provide material support for the elders. This was Timothy's responsibility, not the elders, because Paul charged Timothy, saying, "Let the elders who take the lead well be counted worthy of double honor" (1 Tim. 5:17). This was Timothy's responsibility. When you visit churches in different places, if you see elders who labor in a church and are therefore encountering financial need, those who are Timothys need to cause the local brothers to see that such ones should be given double honor. You need to do this individually.

The Deacons Needing to Bear More Responsibility

Why do the elders come third in the administration of money in the church? In the Bible the administration of money in the church is, of course, the responsibility of the elders. There is no doubt about this. Practically, however, the use of the money in the church is not in the hands of the elders, but in the hands of the deacons. In other words, the use of Jerusalem's money was not in the hands of the twelve apostles, but in the hands of the seven deacons. The fact that the apostles did not attend to tables indicates that they did not manage the use of the money. The principle of administration and the way to administrate are in the hands of the apostles. But when money is actually used, it is in the hands of the seven deacons. Therefore, when arrangements are made for the money, the deacons, not the elders, know the local needs and the needs of the poor. The responsible brothers do not know what the situation is with the brothers in need, but the seven brothers know. Only the seven deacons, not the twelve apostles, are aware of the local expenses. In other words, the use of money is the deacons' business; it is not the elders' business. It is the deacons who manage the local expenses and the giving to the poor.

Therefore, the deacons should also bear more responsibility regarding the supply to the elders. This is my personal opinion. It is very difficult for the elders to do this. It is good if a church can care for the responsible brothers, but the church needs to be aware of their responsibility. At any rate we need to make the church aware of their responsibility.

Here the flesh needs to be terminated. When brothers and sisters give offerings of money, there should not be any personal concerns. When managing money, only God's commandment counts. There should be nothing else, and there should be no personal feelings. You may say that we should give it all to the poor. This means that if it were up to us, we would receive a portion the next time we are poor. Therefore, there cannot be personal feelings. We have given the money to God. It should then be distributed according to what God has decided. First, we should not be indebted to others; all our bills should be paid. Second, we should care for the poor. Third, we should care for the responsible brothers.

The responsible brothers should not take money themselves. The brothers who are deacons should say, "We need to give honor to them." The deacons do this on behalf of the church. In honoring does anybody honor himself? No one honors himself; others are needed for this. Therefore, in this matter the deacons can represent the church to honor them. The brothers who are deacons may say, "I know that at this time a certain brother is having a considerable difficulty. His son needs to go to school this term. We need to consider this matter." The deacons may not propose in other areas, but in this area they may. The elders can speak on any matter, but not on the matter of being honored. They have absolutely no right to speak about this. It is up to the deacons to say something.

This matter is in the hands of the deacons. If we have to call a meeting of the church to decide upon this matter, then we will become Laodicea. It is best to entrust the deacons with this matter so that they can take care of it every week and every month. The time to do this is not fixed. In the Bible the day of settling accounts is not once a month, unlike the tree of life which yields its fruits every month. In Corinthians it says that they settled accounts week by week. The deacons should say that they are going to give a sum of money to a certain elder. The money is in the hands of the deacons. They do not manage the money; they only have custody of the money. They need to say that they represent the church in giving this money to an elder.

In the past the money has been in the hands of the elders. Now we need to change. The elders administrate, but actually the money is in the hands of the deacons. The deacons are the cashiers. In other words, the disbursement of funds is the business of the seven deacons; it is not the business of the twelve apostles. Concerning the elders themselves, the Timothys should indeed always say, "You should care for the needs of the responsible brothers here. They administrate the church. It is wrong for you to treat them in a careless way."

CHAPTER THIRTEEN

ANSWERS TO QUESTIONS

THE MATTER OF THE ELDERS' CHILDREN
BELIEVING IN THE LORD

Question: The Bible indicates that the children of the elders should believe in the Lord. Among us there are a few elders in the church whose children have not yet believed in the Lord. Their children, however, are only in their teens and are not that old. They come to hear the gospel, but they have not yet been saved. What do you think about this?

Answer: I think that your question on the matter of requiring children to believe in the Lord refers to the elders' ability to manage their household. This is the point of emphasis. Therefore, if the children are very young, this does not apply. If a child is very disobedient and rebels against believing, this is a clear indication that the brother has no way to take care of the church. Perhaps he is able to be an apostle, but he does not know how to be an elder. If the young children are not that rebellious or negative and are able to come along with you to listen to the messages, then there is no problem. Of course, when they are young in age, it is impossible to know whether they have genuinely believed. But when they reach a certain age, they should be asked to receive the Lord. I think that the point of emphasis is still on managing one's own household. Therefore, the brother whom you referred to may still be an elder.

THE MEETING BECOMING TOO LARGE
AND THE ORIGINAL RESPONSIBLE BROTHERS
NOT BEING ABLE TO BEAR RESPONSIBILITY

Question: In the past when various localities began to have meetings, the leading brothers there seemed to be able to bear the responsibility. Later, when the number of saints increased, the responsible brothers did not seem to be able to bear the responsibility as before due to their spiritual condition. What should these responsible brothers do?

Answer: In a certain place there may be a group of saints beginning to meet, with some learning to bear the responsibility. According to God's arrangement in the church, when some better ones are brought in, the responsible brothers in that place should be able to allow the better ones to bear the responsibility. The responsible brothers should then listen to these brothers. I hope that we can reach this stage.

Paul said, "We do not have such a custom of being so, neither the churches of God." We do not like to have traditions, but we like to have customs. If one church does things in a certain way, spontaneously other churches will follow. This is a most beautiful thing. Formerly, you were bearing responsibility in a certain locality. Now other brothers have moved to your place. It would be a wonderful thing if you were able to step aside. You may say, "Brother! Come and do it. I will submit to you." This is not being passive. Many people, as soon as they stop bearing responsibility, behave like outsiders and do not care for anything anymore. You should say, "I am willing to help you. You bear the responsibility. You are the one taking the lead." If every church would practice this, such a custom could be established among the churches. When younger brothers encounter those who are more advanced in the Lord than themselves, they should be able to ask them to step forward. The children of God need to learn to recognize those who have higher authority when they meet them. It is not proper to have a confusing situation.

When several brothers go out together or talk together in a room, spontaneously someone will take the lead, and some others will follow. God keeps the order in every matter, whether great or small. God is a God of order. We should also learn to have everything in order, even more so regarding the things of the church. If a brother who bears responsibility knows spontaneously that another brother who has just come in is ahead of him in the Lord, he should lead him to become acquainted with the brothers and gradually withdraw. If he does not recognize that brother, there could be a big problem. If such a custom of order could be established in every locality, it would be a beautiful thing. This is the church of God. Those who have God's authority should always be in the forefront.

Question: What can we do if he does not see?

Answer: I think that sometimes the brothers who are workers traveling through such places should bear more responsibility in such matters. When a brother who is a worker travels through such a place, he should be the one to make a decision according to the situation in that locality. The apostles should look into it and determine who should or should not bear responsibility. It is clear in 3 John that there was a person who had a view different from that of the apostle John. John has one view, and he has another. "Diotrephes, who loves to be first among them, does not receive us" (v. 9). The local brothers were not clear concerning Diotrephes, and thought that he was indeed a person of authority. He loved "to be first among them." He was not willing to receive people, nor was he willing for others to do so. Therefore, John said, "If I come, I will bring to remembrance his works which he does" (v. 10). Hence, strictly speaking, the responsible ones in all the places should be considered by the workers who are reliable in the Lord. The latter should determine who may or may not bear responsibility in a locality.

If we can train the brothers and sisters in various localities with a basic education of knowing authority, it will be easy for them to submit when they go to other places to raise up meetings. The problem today is that the basic training is not sufficient; therefore, this kind of situation exists. Once the basic training is sufficient, the problem will be greatly reduced.

PETER AND PHILIP MOVING INDIVIDUALLY?

Question: Philip went to Samaria by himself, and Peter went to Caesarea by himself. Were these individualistic activities?

Answer: I would like to see these kinds of fruitful individualistic activities. From now on we need to be very careful with this kind of expression—individualistic activities.

There may be many brothers who live together with eight or ten other brothers, yet they can still act individualistically. Not acting individualistically does not mean that we have someone sleeping next to us, or that we have someone eating with us, or that we always buy two tickets when we travel. As long as one has not seen the Body of Christ, he still acts individualistically. He may do things with others physically, but in reality he has not learned to obey authority or to fellowship. This is the kind of person who acts individualistically. Philip could go out by himself, but not act individualistically. Others can go out with eight or ten, yet still act individualistically.

Confronting Authority

The matter of authority is a very wonderful thing in the church. When some workers of God or believers are together, they spontaneously are confronted with the matter of authority. God never does things in a disorderly fashion. Even between two persons, God sets one up as the authority.

Names Having Order

The order of names in the Bible is consistent. There are special reasons when they are not consistent. For example, in the Old Testament God set up Moses as the authority; it was always Moses and Aaron. You cannot reverse the order to have Aaron and Moses. When they were together, one always represented authority and the other represented submission. Even with those sent out by our Lord two by two—those whose names are mentioned—one was before the other. If it was so with two, it is more so with many.

Believing in the Presence of the Holy Spirit

Whenever God's children are together, they should immediately fall in line. This does not mean to line up physically, but that we realize that a brother is in front of us. Since the Lord is working among us, He must have a mouthpiece; therefore, we must believe in God's presence. We should declare, "I believe in the presence of the Lord. I believe in the presence of the Holy Spirit." Consequently, when several brothers have the presence of the Holy Spirit, you must believe that God has a mouthpiece among them.

Not Submitting to a Perfect Person

The reason God's authority cannot be established among His children is that His children are always criticizing others and always asking for perfection. To them there is only one man in the whole world whom they admire—the perfect man. That man has not existed before, does not exist today, and will not exist in the future. Therefore, they cannot submit. They want to submit to a perfect man, but that man does not happen to be around. Therefore, they will not submit to anyone. Yet God does not give His authority to a perfect man; He gives His authority to a man who is being perfected. God gives His authority to a person who is in front of you. This is a basic principle in the Bible. God gives His authority to a brother in front of you.

When God's children are together, they spontaneously should fall into a good order. This is not a matter of organization. It does not mean that when several brothers are together, you need to elect a team leader or a person in charge. But you must realize that even when several go out for a walk on the mountain or when you all gather together, someone will be in front of you. In those five or ten minutes of walking, you need to learn to be a submissive person. Wherever God's children are, regardless of the environment or occasion, there are those in authority and those who should submit. This is a very beautiful thing.

When a person is governed by such a principle, there will be no individualistic activity. When a person does not submit to authority, he will still act individualistically no matter how many others may be with him. What is individualism? Individualism means that you cannot be under authority. When a person is individualistic, he has no way to be under authority. Once he comes under authority, individualism has to go. Once you receive authority, individualism cannot exist.

Not Submitting Selectively

It is not a matter of receiving one authority, nor a matter

of receiving ten authorities; it is a matter of receiving authority.

Let me give you an example. I have used two servants. They started working for me at different times, one earlier than the other. When the first one came to my house, I charged him saying, "There is a basic requirement for you to be a servant—you need to obey. No matter how smart you are, just do whatever I ask you to do." Later, I also told the other servant, "You need to learn to obey. You need to listen to me, and you also need to listen to the servant who came before you." However, the servant who came later obeyed all of my words, but he did not obey the words of the servant who came earlier. He always tried to find ways to point out the mistakes of the other servant. Do you think that this person submitted to authority?

What is submission to authority? Submission to authority does not mean choosing the person to whom you will submit. If you choose the person to whom you will submit, you do not know authority. He who knows authority recognizes it whenever he encounters it. When he encounters it, he knows he should submit. If you cannot submit, it proves that you have never known authority. You may have submitted to man, but not to authority. At best you merely fear a man, and when you meet him you obey him. You have never been under authority because you have never known authority. Authority is not a matter of one place or another place. There is authority in every place and on every occasion. Regardless of where one may be, he who knows authority recognizes it whenever he encounters it.

When a person is under authority, individualism cannot exist. If you stand on the ground of individualism, you will have no way to submit yourself to authority. This is a very important matter as far as spiritual principles are concerned. A person needs to learn to know authority. For Christians it is not a matter of who a person is. Christians should submit to authority whenever we encounter it.

Seeking Fellowship

Individualism cannot exist if one seeks fellowship. With

individualism one always tries to maintain his individual spiritual life before God, his individual visions before God, and his individual work before God. He is always an individual; it is not easy for him to seek fellowship. This is the problem among us. Such a person does not seek fellowship, but struggles and labors by himself. Many children of God today can say only in words that they cannot do without other brothers or that they must have the church in order to live. Actually, many can live without the church and without fellowship. This proves that they are individualistic. If a person receives the principle of fellowship and the principle of the Body only in concept, yet in actuality lives and works by himself, has a spiritual life without fellowship, and does the work of the Lord without fellowship, then this person has never been broken before God. He is altogether an individualistic person. Fellowship is versus individualism. It is not what you say about fellowship; rather, it is a matter of whether fellowship is a part of your life, whether you really cannot live or work without fellowship. One day God will bring you to this stage. I feel that this is the greatest step.

Not Merely a Matter
of Lacking Faithfulness and Faith

When many people come to an impasse, they only consider that there are problems with their faith or faithfulness; they do not consider that there is a problem with their fellowship. The education which many people have received in the past and the books which many have read instruct people to be faithful, to believe, and to submit directly to God. Therefore, a problem occurs when they are unable to get through. When they cannot get through in their personal lives, they always consider that they themselves have a problem, that their faith has a problem, or that they are lacking in faithfulness. This is right, but many only see that their failures and difficulties are due to problems in their personal faith, their personal faithfulness, or their personal submission. They do not see that there is something else in the Bible called fellowship. If there are problems with fellowship, they can also arrive at the same point of failure and difficulty.

Many people's problems have nothing to do with the matter of faith or believing in God, but the matter of fellowship. Sometimes the Lord must allow this kind of person to struggle in his faith, faithfulness, and submission so that he reaches a point in his Christian life where he simply cannot believe or submit no matter how hard he tries. Perhaps he will then realize that he cannot make it simply as one member, nor can he make it merely by his union with Christ. He must be joined with the Body of Christ in order to get through. Perhaps he will then begin to see that he needs the help of other Christians in order to make it. Many have not yet been brought on this way; they are still walking on the way of individualism, laboring by themselves. It is God's great mercy to bring a person to a point where he cannot get through, and where his eyes are opened to see that while submission, faith, and faithfulness do not suffice, fellowship does suffice.

This is a great revelation! One day God's children will be brought to a stage where all their ways are exhausted, and where they see that even such a great item as faith does not avail. Faith is not a small matter, and we should not despise it. Faith, faithfulness, and submission are all great matters. However, one day you will reach a point that even when all these conditions are fulfilled, you still cannot get through. Faith, faithfulness, and submission to God are all weighty matters in the Bible. But even with these weighty things, you still have no way to get through until your eyes are opened one day and you begin to realize that fellowship is also a great matter. Without fellowship, you cannot get through. Only a person who has passed through this pathway before God can escape individualism, not doing things individualistically. Those who only know the doctrine of fellowship or the doctrine of the Body of Christ can still be individualistic for the rest of their lives. They can believe in the doctrine of fellowship in a very individualistic way. God needs to bring them on a path where everything is exhausted, where the way is impassable, and where their problems still cannot be solved even though they continue to believe, be faithful, and submit. When God gives them a little light one day, they will see that their problem was actually in the matter of fellowship. Then their individualism will depart.

Peter Seeking Fellowship under Authority

When Peter went to Caesarea by himself, he did not go individualistically. He had fellowship. When Peter went from Joppa to Caesarea, he took the brothers from Joppa with him. He was always under authority and always seeking fellowship. Therefore, as soon as he returned to Jerusalem, he told the brothers what had happened. Although the job had been done, he still sought fellowship.

Philip Being Met by the Holy Spirit

When Philip went to Samaria, he was one who submitted himself under authority. Otherwise, the Holy Spirit would not have called him to the wilderness. All those whom the Holy Spirit has met are those who are still going on. Everything in the church is arranged and regulated by the Holy Spirit. The Head of the church is Christ, but the operation of the Head is through His Spirit. When the Holy Spirit brought Philip to the wilderness, he was still under authority.

Not a Matter of the Number of People

Individualism is not a matter of one person or two; it is not a question of more people or less people. Individualism is a matter of whether one is under authority and whether one has the fellowship of the Body. Today some brothers may go out with several others, but these brothers can still be completely individualistic. When you go down from the mountain to work, you may say that you are standing in the position of the Body to learn to serve, yet if five of you are still five persons, and ten of you are still ten persons, you have failed completely before God. That is not fellowship. Fellowship is not a matter of how many people are in the room, the number of people who sit beside you, or whether anyone accompanies you as you go out. The Bible emphasizes two persons going out together so that there may be fellowship concerning things. But this does not mean that when there are more people, there is fellowship, and when there are fewer people, there is no fellowship.

Today, God's children should know these two basic lessons. First, they need to know authority and submit to authority. Second, they should treasure the fellowship of the children of God. They should seek the fellowship of life and the supply of life from others so that they can go forward. Only when these two lessons are present can we be free from individualism. When these two lessons are absent, immediately individualism becomes present.

The Basic Principle of
Having Two or More Persons

In the Bible the principle of workers going out to work is that of at least two by two. For example, when Paul went out to work, there were at least two persons. There might have been an exception to this principle in Philip's going to Samaria. If a man is under authority and lives in fellowship, even if he has one exception, he still does not damage the basic principle.

This does not mean that having many people going out is sufficient. If you are not in oneness, even if there are ten brothers going out to work together, it is useless. Therefore, when you go to Wen-Shu or Tsingtao, it is not a matter of electing someone to be a group leader. This is not something done by the church. Rather, spontaneously you realize that there is a person in front of you, and that you need to listen to him. Spontaneously, you learn submission and fellowship. Many people will become as one man, as one body going out. In this there is no individualism. Otherwise, if you have one person, it is called one-person individualism; if you have ten persons, it is called ten-person individualism. The more persons there are, the more individualisms there are. Thus, you will be proposing a work based upon multiple individualisms. In the past you might have believed in personal individualism; today you believe in plural individualisms. If this is the case, this is not the Body of Christ.

We need to know what the Body of Christ is. The Body of Christ is one in life and submits under authority. This authority can be manifested among any group of God's children. Each one needs to learn to stand in his place; then there will not be any problems. In such a condition one should not humble himself deliberately, nor should he be so concerned for himself. Rather, he should learn to accept man's instruction and opinion and learn to submit to authority. As everyone stands in his own place, all will see that this way is proper. Perhaps all the problems are due to individualism. This is the whole problem and the greatest problem.

THE APPOINTMENT OF THE ELDERS AND THE APOSTLES BEING ELDERS

Question: According to the Epistles to Timothy, the elders must be appointed by people like Paul, Timothy, or Titus. Peter and John were elders in Jerusalem. Did James appoint them? Or were they appointed by themselves when necessary?

Answer: I believe that all the elders need to be appointed; therefore, I mentioned that all the elders must be appointed by the workers when they are in their midst. I want you to pay special attention to what Paul said to the elders of the church in Ephesus. This church was different from the church at the center of the work. However, they shared the same principle, which is that the Holy Spirit has placed the elders as overseers of the whole flock. Therefore, when the workers and apostles appoint elders in other places, they must have a desire, a seeking, and prayer before God, with the assurance that the persons whom they appoint are the persons whom the Holy Spirit appoints. Otherwise, the problems will be great. The Holy Spirit appoints one person, but the one you appoint is another person. The problem this gives to the church is too great. Therefore, as each goes down from the mountain, no brother can become loose or casual in appointing elders in other places. Paul had the boldness to say in Ephesus that the Holy Spirit had appointed them as elders. Paul did not say that he had appointed them but that the Holy Spirit had appointed them. He had considerable confidence to say that the Holy Spirit had appointed them. Therefore, we need to be in fear and trembling. We are afraid of people who are too bold. We should be in fear and trembling. We have to see that the responsibility of deciding who are and who are not elders is very heavy. We must have adequate consideration and prayer before God. Only those who are appointed by the Holy Spirit are useful. Otherwise, they will be useless and will sooner or later be problems.

The positions of Peter and John in Jerusalem were quite clear because they were apostles. The elders are appointed by the apostles. Peter the apostle appointed Peter the elder, and John the apostle appointed John the elder because this responsibility was in the hands of the apostles, and at the same time there was a local need. Perhaps, among those apostles, they might have all felt that at least these two should bear the local responsibility at the same time. Therefore, they both became elders in Jerusalem. Toward the end James had passed away, and the other James remained. In the church in Jerusalem, he was definitely in the forefront. Perhaps Peter and John were not appointed by him, but I dare not say. However, there hardly was a problem for Peter and John to be elders because they were already apostles.

BEING SENT MORE
IN THE ELEMENT OF FELLOWSHIP

Question: Peter and John went to Samaria, and the Bible says that the apostles in Jerusalem sent them. Paul and Barnabas went, and the Bible says that the brothers sent them. Why is this?

Answer: In this kind of sending, there is fellowship. You dare not say that there was authority, but at least there was fellowship.

The Story of Peter and John

There were twelve apostles in Jerusalem. The matter of Samaria was brought to Jerusalem. Jerusalem knew the situation in Samaria, and they also saw that the believers in Samaria had not received the Holy Spirit. Philip only did a part of the work; he did not do the work thoroughly. So Jerusalem felt that Peter and John should go. Perhaps, while twelve or more than twelve brothers were waiting and praying together, Peter and John felt that they should go, and the rest of the brothers also felt that they should go. So they sent Peter and John to Samaria. This is a very beautiful picture. I dare not say that the matter of authority had no part, but I feel that the matter of authority did not occupy a major role; the greater part was the principle of fellowship. Suppose while there are a number of sisters eating together, they feel that one among them should go to a certain sister's home. This is not a matter of authority; rather, everyone considers together who should go. The principle of fellowship has a greater part than the principle of authority. I do not say that it has no part, but I say that the greater part is the part of fellowship.

The Story of Paul and Silas

It was the same with Paul and Silas. In Thessalonica they encountered danger. Paul was imprisoned, but later he was released. After he was released, when the brothers were together, he was sent by them to Berea. Here we clearly see that in this certain brother's home, the home of Jason, they were praying, seeking, and considering their future. As a result they said that Paul and Silas should not continue living there and that for them to remain there would be very difficult. The brothers felt to send them perhaps to Berea. Therefore, in this instance, there was also the flavor of the fellowship of the brothers and sisters.

You will remember that I mentioned yesterday that Paul had two things in his work. When Paul sent Timothy, very often it was through fellowship, because Timothy often could not see clearly. It is not that I use authority to tell you to go; rather, it is that I fellowship the Lord's desire with you so that you can walk more properly. Perhaps you did not see the importance of fellowship yesterday. Today you need to see these two aspects. Very often it is not just a matter of authority but a matter of fellowship. You need fellowship because perhaps you have not seen, no one has made a decision, and you yourself do not know what to do. Perhaps the brothers made the decision, or perhaps Paul made the decision. Even if Paul made the decision, it was not through authority but through the fellowship with the house of Jason.

In Thessalonica it was very clear: The brothers were together, Paul and Silas were in danger, and the Jews wanted to arrest them. What should they do? The brothers felt that they should still go forward, so they went forward. It seems that they were discussing together, and they went out. Therefore, the brothers sending them to Berea was simply a fellowship in the Lord. What was the result? The result was very good. The Bereans were better than the Thessalonians because they were willing to study the Bible.

I do not say that there was no authority, but I say that the element of fellowship was greater. It is possible that there was no element of authority. However, there was fellowship. Paul sent others many times. Even though Paul was a brother in the lead, you still have to admit that there was also an element of fellowship. There are two basic principles in the coordination of God's work: authority and fellowship. When both principles are present, it is the highest leading and the most perfect coordination.

The Words of the Holy Spirit Being Spoken through the Prophets

Question: What would you say concerning the sending in Acts 13? Verse 2 says, "The Holy Spirit said." Where is the fellowship? Or is there something else?

Answer: At the time of the apostles, the words of the Holy Spirit could come from the mouths of the prophets. Among those brothers there were prophets who rose up and said, "Set apart for Me now Barnabas and Saul." Perhaps there was not only one person, but two or three, witnessing what the Holy Spirit was doing.

ONLY TWO CENTERS BEING MENTIONED IN ACTS

Question: Jerusalem and Antioch did not have much difference. In just over ten years, how could there already be two beginnings?

Answer: It was only a period of ten years. The Bible did record two beginnings. However, Philippians says that there were still many people preaching the gospel although their way was not proper. They clearly were not from Jerusalem or Antioch, but they were another group of people who initiated another beginning. By this we may know that there were many beginnings at that time.

I think that the record of the Holy Spirit in Acts and in Revelation 2 and 3 is the same. There were many churches in Asia, but only seven were selected to receive the epistles. Obviously, Ephesus and Colossae were both in Asia, but only Ephesus was mentioned, not Colossae. Clearly the condition of Colossae was better than that of Ephesus because Ephesus had already fallen to the extent of leaving the first love and Colossae had not. For the sake of applying the teaching, the Lord chose Ephesus. Because the Lord wanted to match the teaching with history, He chose seven. I believe that all the history in Acts is for teaching; therefore, many people were omitted. Hence, we are clear concerning Peter in Jerusalem and Paul in Antioch. There could have been many other beginnings. History shows us that a group of apostles went to Africa. According to the tradition of the church, Thomas went to India. Each way was separate, and the Bible did not bother to mention them at all. Therefore, we cannot say that in Acts there were only two centers; we can only say that the Holy Spirit only mentioned two centers.

This is also like the Holy Spirit only mentioning Adam, Eve, Abel, and Cain. It does not mean that there were only four persons in the world at that time. What this means is that only what is useful to teaching is recorded, and what is not useful to teaching is not recorded. Philippians 1 shows us that many gospel preachers went out. Many of them may have had situations similar to Paul's.